~wn.

Discover your roots

Discover
your roots

52 brilliant ideas for exploring your family and local history

Paul Blake & Maggie Loughran

brilliantideas

CAREFUL NOW

We hope you will enjoy the brilliant ideas contained in this book. Use the information wisely and you will find yourself gradually building up an interesting collection of facts, documents and images about your family, house or local area. While we do our best to provide you with the most up to the minute resources it's obvious that information is not a static thing, especially where the world wide web is concerned – for this we apologise but we can't be held responsible. It's your life so sharpen your pencil, put on your sleuthing hat and get out there and enjoy yourself.

Copyright © The Infinite Ideas Company Limited, 2006

The right of Paul Blake and Maggie Loughran to be identified as the authors of this book has been asserted in accordance with the Copyright, Designs and Patents Act 1988

First published in 2006 by
The Infinite Ideas Company Limited
36 St Giles
Oxford, OX1 3LD
United Kingdom
www.infideas.com

Reprinted 2006

A CIP catalogue record for this book is available from the British Library

ISBN 10: 1-904902-67-7   ISBN 13: 978-1-904902-67-6

Brand and product names are trademarks or registered trademarks of their respective owners.

Designed by Baseline Arts Ltd, Oxford
Typeset by Sparks, Oxford
Printed by TJ International, Cornwall

Brilliant ideas

Brilliant features xiii

Introduction xiv

1 **What's in a name?** 1
Taylor, Townsend, Thompson: we all have a name but where did it come from and what does it mean?

2 **Who told you that?** 5
Family stories abound but discovering which parts are true and which are false is a problem. The answer is to use first-hand accounts as the foundation of your investigations.

3 **Show and tell** 9
From old boxes under the bed to dirt-encrusted suitcases in the attic, we all have collections of memorabilia, ephemera and documents relating to the history of our homes and family.

4 **Is there anybody out there?** 13
You're not alone – there are countless others trying to discover more about themselves or their communities. Contacting them can only help you with your own researches.

5 **Truth and lies** 17
By asking questions, particularly of your older relatives, you could get vital clues about your family's past. However, don't rely completely on family stories before you've cross-checked them with other sources.

6   **Join the club** 21
Local history societies and family history societies abound in all parts of the world. Their journals and books are a rich source of help and advice if you know how to use them effectively.

7   **Hatches, matches and despatches** 27
Since the mid-nineteenth century, the government has been officially recording births, marriages and deaths. Join us to glean the most from these records.

8   **Let no man put asunder** 31
Not as common as it is now, but the best of intentions have often ended in separation and divorce in the past. And if not the latter, then wife-selling or bigamy may have resulted.

9   **All the news that's fit to print** 35
Newspapers are a fantastic resource for the local and family historian. They are full of information – both about people and places – that you will rarely find recorded anywhere else.

10 **Did he fall or was he pushed?** 41
Our most intriguing ancestors are dead ones, particularly if their end was of the sticky variety. Coroners' records and newspapers may reveal all.

11 **Writ in stone**.. 47
Slabs, brasses, headstones, memorial gardens, crematoria and churchyards can all bring the dead back to life for you – metaphorically speaking, that is.

12 **Reading, 'riting, 'rithmetic** 51
The provision of free education for all was part of the push for social reform and improvement of the masses. Now it also provides history hunters with a new source of information.

13 **The sense of the census** 55
One of the most important – and easily accessible – primary resources for local and
family historians is the census. Learning how to interpret it properly will pay handsome
dividends.

14 **Location, location, location** 59
Just as now, in previous centuries anyone wanting to know the location of a local plumber
or undertaker, or even the address of an acquaintance, would turn to a local directory.
You can turn those same pages.

15 **Votes and voters** 65
Although not all of us were able to vote until 1929, if you know who could vote, where,
and when, then another potential source of information about your ancestors becomes
available.

16 **Taxing the community** 69
Taxation is as old as time, and that's just as well from the historians' perspective because
tax records offer a wealth of information about the lives of our ancestors.

17 **How does the land lie?** 73
The maps and plans of Britain are a cornucopia of landscape information. Plot the geographical changes in your community and see how it grows.

18 **Become a where wolf** 77
Begin your prowl and discover what's found where within the giant labyrinth of archives,
libraries and record repositories.

19 **Files, formats and family trees** 83
Clarity, Convenience and Completeness are the golden rules for organizing your research.
Living by them might be difficult, but the benefits are well worth the effort.

20 **Fancy a date?** 89
All dates are not the same so it is important that you understand the old dating practices
in order to date documents correctly.

21 **On the move** 93
Follow the branches of your family's migrations – they may stretch further and wider
than you think.

22 **Open the doors and see the people** 97
For centuries, the Church has kept registers of baptisms, marriages and burials. They can
very effectively open up a window on the lives of our forebears.

23 **Where there's a will** 103
Wills have a singular importance, not least because of the detail they frequently contain
about family, relationships, property and place of burial.

24 **Inghamites, Swedenborgians, Muddletonians and others** 109
If we were all the same, it would be a dull world – and when it comes to religion, it's no
different. Nonconformist ancestors can add even more depth to your roots.

25 **Daddy, what did *you* do in the war?** 113
Most of our parents and grandparents played a part in the twentieth century wars, even
as civilians. Find out what part it was that they played.

26 **For king and country** 119
If not 'tinker or tailor' then possibly 'soldier or sailor'. In yesteryear, almost every family
has been represented in its country's armed forces. Hence, a good place to look for
ancestors.

27 **Apprenticeships and apprentices** 123
Apprenticeship indentures can be an invaluable source for discovering the origins of a
tradesman or artisan among your ancestors.

28 **Trades and occupations** 127
Were your ancestors higglers or badgers; labourers or lacemakers; clockmakers or carmen; or even working in the 'oldest profession'? Find out.

29 **Professions and professionals** 131
Architects, doctors, clerics, surgeons, MPs, lawyers, dentists and their ilk: professionals are usually far easier to trace than ancestors who were labourers.

30 **Get if off your chest** 137
Parish chests are a rich supply of information rarely found anywhere else. They can give you a fantastic insight into the life of your forebears.

31 **Arms and the man** 141
Heraldry is all around us – on inn signs, in stained-glass church windows and as hatchments (armorial bearings of the dead) – and perhaps on the spoons in your cutlery drawer.

32 **Manors maketh man** 145
Lords and labourers all contributed to the extraordinary records of the manorial courts, which can reveal the history of communities from the twelfth century.

33 **Crime and punishment** 149
For the family historian, crime really does pay. Criminal ancestors left an extensive paper trail, allowing you to uncover a tremendous amount of information about them.

34 **Let's get out of here** 153
Emigration has generated a wide diversity of records, which, due to their very origins, need to be hunted for in a number of different places.

35 **Aliens in the family** 157
Your ancestors may have been among the refugees, merchants and entrepreneurs who, over the centuries, decided that the grass was greener in Britain and made the move.

36 **Helical help**..161

Not too long ago, you were the child of your father according to your mother. Today, genetics can help in determining our origins, but it's still not the great revealer that many believe.

37 **Digitise your data** 165

You don't have to be swamped by bits of paper. Get that scanner working overtime and let your computer take the strain.

38 **Publishing on the web**..169

Keep it to yourself if you want, but you can share the results of your sleuthing with the outside world using the World Wide Web – and its fun to do, too.

39 **Grave responsibilities** 173

Many Victorian cemeteries are places of outstanding historical interest, with fine examples of Victorian gothic funerary architecture. They offer great insights into past times.

40 **Creative scrapbooking**...177

Have you ever thought of producing a book to pass down through the generations: a book of few words but many illustrations? It's well worth considering.

41 **The truly obsessed**...181

For some, gathering every reference to a particular surname or place is their *raison d'être*. It may not be your idea of fun, but don't knock them because they could help you.

42 **The Lloyd George Domesday** 185

Often referred to as the 'Second Domesday Survey', this is one of the most easily accessible and helpful sources for twentieth-century research.

43 **The National Farm Survey** 189
During the Second World War, every farm or similar holding of five acres or more was
surveyed. Owners, occupiers and the state of cultivation are all detailed. Those details
are there for you now.

44 **Bricks and mortar** 193
The architectural heritage of the British Isles is one of the richest in the world. Even your
own home will have a story to tell about the history of your area.

45 **Plots and plans**...197
In the absence of photographs, there are many other records that will give you a strong
flavour of what your house, or other particular building of interest, was like in the past.

46 **Families in focus** 201
Discovering family photographs is enormously satisfying, but what do you actually see?
Open your mind to *all* of what they are really telling you.

47 **Places in perspective**...205
Many elements of the landscape are invisible. Recognise the clues, though, and you'll
discover your surroundings far beyond your normal pedestrian point of view.

48 **A rue with a view** 209
See your street and community through the eyes of those residents of earlier times by
discovering contemporary postcards of the area. They provide a fascinating snapshot of
the past.

49 **Cameras are not just for holidays!**..213
Or how to make sure you create your own modern-day photo archive.

50 **Diversify – doing your own thing**..217
There are plenty of opportunities to follow your own interests and keep your passion
burning. Research what really fascinates you, not what the books tell you that you
should be doing.

51 **Get Googling**...223
The internet is a vast collection of information and it grows remorselessly by the day, by more
than a million pages. To get the best from it, you need to learn to use it effectively.

52 **How to avoid becoming an anorak**..227
Being an avid history chaser doesn't mean you inevitably become the local bore who
everybody avoids. Follow these simple rules and you can remain quite normal.

Brilliant resources...231
Useful contact addresses and websites

The end 234

Where it's at 236
Index

Brilliant features

Each chapter of this book is designed to provide you with an inspirational idea that you can read quickly and put into practice straight away.

Throughout you'll find four features that will help you get right to the heart of the idea:

- *Here's an idea for you ...* Take it on board and give it a go – right here, right now. Get an idea of how well you're doing so far.

- *Try another idea ...* If this idea looks like a life-changer then there's no time to lose. *Try another idea ...* will point you straight to a related tip to enhance and expand on the first.

- *Defining idea ...* Words of wisdom from masters and mistresses of the art, plus some interesting hangers-on.

- *How did it go?* If at first you do succeed, try to hide your amazement. If, on the other hand, you don't, then this is where you'll find a Q and A that highlights common problems and how to get over them.

Introduction

'The past is a foreign country; they do things differently there.'

The oft-quoted opening lines of L P Hartley's *The Go-between* usually produce a smile of acceptance or a nod of agreement, but rarely the question 'So, different how, then?'

No one really needs to look too far to discover vestiges of the past. They can be found in houses, in snapshots in family photo albums, even in the shops we go to and the places where we spend our leisure time. Too often, the apparently ordinary or trivial aspects of history are ignored in favour of the grand monuments, the great characters or the momentous events. Yet it is the ordinary and the trivial that can reveal a wealth of information about life in the past. If they are overlooked for too long there is the danger that they will disappear for ever.

Our heritage is a rich one. All of us experience some sense of the past every day. We see it all about us: a Victorian pub, a deserted factory, the local war memorial, the local common, even in the black and white films from the thirties and forties shown on the television. The past is in towns, in the countryside, at the seaside. Too often we hardly notice it, if at all.

Whether you think you are interested in local history, family history or community history, the truth is that you are in fact interested in all three – and probably much else besides. All history is about people: after all, family history is about people in places and local history is about places with people. To over-define either does neither a service.

Your past, the lives of your ancestors, was touched by national and local economics, religion, war and probably by disease, pestilence and the weather. You should not be expecting to tell the whole story; just that part that affected you and yours. If this book is different it is because it has tried not to restrict itself to any one discipline but introduce a whole range of ideas for you to think about and try to use.

Of all the various avenues of historical study that there are, local and family history have the advantage of being the most accessible to the amateur sleuth. No formal qualifications are needed and the non-expert is not overly disadvantaged by not having an academic or scholarly background. Enthusiasm, supplemented by a little reading, is all that is required. To learn that bit more and meet like-minded folk, take advantage of the adult education classes that are certain to be taking place near to you, and join a local society. The difference between professional and amateur researchers, between full-time and part-time researchers, pales into insignificance compared with the difference between good and bad research, the only difference that really matters.

Researching your past begins at home. It begins with simple questions, such as: who were my great-grandparents? when was my house built? The answers to such basic questions are usually easily found and for research in the nineteenth and twentieth centuries no special skills are required. From such simple questions, and their answers, will hopefully come the desire for a wider knowledge of your own personal past. Answers produce more questions: where did my ancestors live? what did they do? why did they come here, go there? what was here before this house? why is my local hostelry called the Grosvenor Arms?

The past starts now. There is often a desire, perhaps resulting from a misconception, that researching the past means going back as far as possible as quickly as possible. Nothing is further from the truth. The 'whom begat whom begat whom …' syndrome is thankfully virtually moribund. If that is your bag, don't let us stop you. But you will have a much greater satisfaction by, as it is usually gruesomely put, putting the flesh on the bones as you go. Yes, do what you want to do, but tracing your family back to 1543 doesn't impress too many people these days and it is usually the uninformed who now ask the question 'how far back have you got?' It is how much and how well, not how far, that is important.

Lastly, we need to remember the words of John Berger, London-born writer and essayist (1926–): 'We are in our time and they are in theirs.' Tempting as it might be to judge and condemn, based on today's morality, ethics and beliefs, we have to respect the fact that the past was different. The past and our forebears made us what we are – but now is not then, and we are not they. What is strange, unacceptable and sometimes repugnant to us was the way of the world to them. The rules and expectations were different.

The past may initially appear to be inaccessible, kept remote by an impenetrable force-field of time: we may occasionally only see vague representations of it, as through frosted glass. However, the past is there for us to unearth. That past is our past and hopefully this little book will inspire you to undertake that voyage of discovery.

1

What's in a name?

Taylor, Townsend, Thompson: we all have a name but where did it come from and what does it mean?

Tracing your past, on the whole, involves looking at lists of names: that is how we recognise our ancestors when we find them.

The sources from which our names are derived are almost endless: nicknames, physical attributes, counties, trades, heraldic charges, and almost every object known to mankind.

When communities were small, each person was identifiable by a single personal name or nickname, but as the population increased it gradually became necessary to identify people further – leading to names such as Henry the baker, John the long, Giles from Sutton, Ann of the hill and Henry son of William.

It was the Norman barons who introduced the concept of surnames into England, and then the practice gradually spread. So trades, nicknames, places of origin, and fathers' names became fixed surnames – names such as Fletcher, Redhead, Green,

Here's an idea for you... **Much has been written about the meanings of surnames. Go to your local library and you will find several volumes, many quite weighty, to put you on the right track. Names are a great thing to 'Google' too, and this can be a very rewarding approach. There are also several specialist websites dedicated to the subject, and these will almost certainly cover most of the names in which you are interested.**

Wilkins and Johnson. Initially, these names were changed or dropped at will, but eventually they began to stick and to get passed on. By 1400 most English families, and those from Lowland Scotland, had adopted the use of these hereditary surnames.

New surnames continued to be formed long after 1400, and immigrants brought in new ones. Many Irish and Highland Scottish names derive from Gaelic personal names, as do those of the Welsh, who only began to adopt the English system of surnames following the union of the two countries in 1536.

The study of surnames is obviously vital to the process of ancestor tracing. However, it is easy to place excessive importance on the family surname in the belief that knowing its meaning or origin may somehow help in tracing your family tree. This is all happened too far back to be helpful in researching family origins, although the study of a particular surname may be useful when the investigation points to an area where it appears often. So you can see that only by tracing a particular family line, possibly back to the fourteenth century or beyond, will you discover which version of a surname is yours. It might be interesting to know that your surname may be derived from a place, such as Lancaster, for example, or an occupation, such as Weaver, but this is not necessarily of relevance to your family history.

Where a study of a particular surname may be of benefit in family history research is when investigation into the distribution of a name points to an area of the country or a county where it is particularly dense. Many have changed their names or adopted an alias at some time in the past, possibly for some legal reason, such as complying with a request in a will, or simply because the new name was preferred to the old one. This highlights the fact that although surnames are an essential part of family history research, it is all too easy to place excessive reliance on their origin and meaning.

Out there are individuals and groups who are collecting every occurrence of a particular surname, and its variant spellings. If your name is amongst those then you may be onto a winner. Check out IDEA 41, *The truly obsessed*.

Try another idea…

So, only by tracing a particular family line will you discover which version of a name is yours. It is more important to be aware that both surnames and forenames are subject to variations in spelling, and not only in the distant past. Standardised spelling did not really arrive until the nineteenth century, and even in the present day variations occur, often by accident through administrative errors – how much of your post has your name spelt incorrectly, for example?

**'O Romeo, Romeo, wherefore art thou Romeo?
Deny thy father and refuse thy name,
Or, if thou wilt not, be but sworn my love,
And I'll no longer be a Capulet.'**
WILLIAM SHAKESPEARE
(*Romeo and Juliet*)

Defining idea…

How did it go?

Q **Are you saying that the surname I have now may not be the same as my grandfather's, or his father's or his father's ...?**

A *Absolutely right. Thankfully, most of our forebears were content with the name they had inherited, even if it erred towards the comical. However, so long as there is no intent to defraud, avoid any legal obligation and if not because of any criminal intent, English citizens under Common Law could and can use whatever surname they choose, without going through any formal process of change of name. I had a mother and daughter in a family history class I ran a few years ago. The mother was Mrs White and the daughter was Miss Whyte – she just wanted to be different!*

Q **Are there any other ways my ancestors might have changed their names?**

A *It is important to be aware that both surnames and forenames are subject to variations in spelling, and not only in the distant past. In addition, before the time when divorce became easier and more acceptable, people often took their partners' names to give the appearance of marriage or of legitimacy for their children.*

2

Who told you that?

Family stories abound but discovering which parts are true and which are false is a problem. The answer is to use first-hand accounts as the foundation of your investigations.

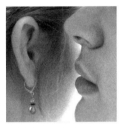

There is usually some truth in any family tradition but, if not in all of it, which bit? The skill you need to develop is identifying the hard facts from the flights of fancy. What would you make of the example below?

'An Irish cousin told me that my Great-aunt Christina, an expert lacemaker, made the wedding veil for Queen Victoria's daughter, and came to London from Limerick in Ireland to deliver it.'

History surrounds us all: it's all of our 'yesterdays', our everyday memories and experiences. Every day, people tell each other 'stories' of what's been happening to them or what they have 'been up to'. This kind of history – the type that each and every one of us collects throughout life – is called oral history. Some people have been involved in momentous historical events, like world wars, or attended an Olympic games, but many others haven't. However, regardless of age or importance, we all have interesting and exciting experiences to share, stories to tell.

More importantly, historical documents and books cannot always tell us everything about our past. Often they concentrate on famous people and major events and tend to miss out the story of 'everyday folk', often neglecting the multicultural aspect of modern society. Oral history fills in the gaps, but because memories die when people do, history can be easily lost – how many of us have photographs that include unknown faces at an event long forgotten in the mists of time? So it is important that our memories be preserved for all time as a permanent record of how we used to live, work and feel.

All memories are a mixture of facts and opinions, and both are important. The way in which people make sense of their lives is valuable historical evidence in itself. Few of us are good at remembering dates – we tend to 'telescope' two similar events into a single memory or confuse dates and places or even generations. So, when we talk to people while investigating our history, it is important to get them to tell us about direct personal experiences – eyewitness testimony – rather than things that might have been heard second-hand.

Here's an idea for you... If recording memories for a specific project, it's useful to do some background research first. Have a look in your local library or record office at any books, maps, old newspapers or listings that might be relevant to the discussion you're about to have.

The story of the wedding veil is a glowing example of what happens when a memory is passed down over several generations. With a little basic investigation, I discovered that my Great-aunt Christina was only 4 years old when Queen Victoria's fifth and young-est daughter was married in 1885, so was too young to have worked on her wedding veil. However, in 1905 a granddaughter of Queen Victoria married into the Swedish Royal family wearing a veil made from Limerick lace, so there may be a little bit of truth in the story …

Most of us have lives full of hustle and bustle, but hopefully can still find the time to get together with other family members, even if it's only at Christmas and other high days and holidays. All family reunions should be seen as an ideal opportunity to catch up, to chat and to reminisce about things that happened long ago, or perhaps not so long ago. This type of gathering can also be a great time to collect and share family stories. Certainly one of the most cherished gifts one can give or receive is a family heirloom, along with the story of the people whose lives surrounded it. Such exchanges leave everyone inspired to find out more.

Do remember, though, that all information is open to question if it's second-hand. Everything needs to be properly checked for accuracy and confirmed wherever possible.

Most of our parents and grandparents have been embroiled in the major wars and conflicts of the twentieth century, either in the forces or just as importantly 'keeping the home fires burning'. So now is the time to ask just what your family's involvement was. Get some pointers from IDEA 25, *What did you do in the war, daddy?*

Try another idea…

'There was never yet an uninteresting life. Such a thing is an impossibility. Inside of the dullest exterior, there is a drama, a comedy, and a tragedy.'
MARK TWAIN (1835-1910)

Defining idea…

Q **I don't seem to get the opportunity at any family gatherings to sit down and really talk to people. What can I do about this?**

A   Why not organise your own family reunion and get other interested family members to help you discover what memories are held or what family heirlooms, photographs or other family documents have survived? Make the most of technology: for spontaneous 'moments', purchase some disposable cameras and hand them out to volunteer guests, but don't forget to collect them at the end of the day. Video the day's event, which gives you the option of both pictures and sounds. Capture still shots to use from your video if you can. Use the latest of innovations to capture images and sound. Create your very own history archive.

Q **What if I don't just want to sit down and record my family's memories of other family members. Any other suggestions?**

A   There are many alternative windows on the past. These could be your own home, the place where you work, your school, how people used to cook – anything. Basically, you pick a topic to ask people about: for example, memories of childhood, leisure, politics, religion or women's experience in wartime, or memories of coming to Britain as a migrant. There are many such projects that are already ongoing, and a wealth of information deposited in Sound Archives, including the recordings of many famous people that you may want to listen to before you start your own project.

3

Show and tell

From old boxes under the bed to dirt-encrusted suitcases in the attic, we all have collections of memorabilia, ephemera and documents relating to the history of our homes and family.

Building up a full picture of your family's past as you go along is as important as discovering who your ancestors were. It is amazing how much can be found in papers secreted about the house or in the memories of your relatives.

So, start rummaging for family papers and memorabilia, and recording the memories of those who now possess them. What have you and your family got stored away? Start with yourself before moving on to your nearest and dearest – and remember too that it may not be the near or the dear that have the most useful stuff. Go through the trunks in the attic and the boxes under the stairs. Disregard nothing: it may be meaningless now but after a bit of investigation it may hold that vital piece of evidence you need. You are after anything you can find: letters, medals, photographs, a family Bible, birthday books, funeral cards, old postcards, birth, marriage and death certificates, baptism certificates, school reports, newspaper cuttings, details of a family grave – anything. You are after facts and you are after clues.

Your big personal breakthrough will come when you realise that most of the apparently insignificant papers and artefacts collecting dust have, as it were, a life beyond themselves. Every item you will come across is what it is – but almost certainly it will also be a clue or clues to further sources of research. Take First World War campaign medals, for example: these are going to be engraved with the recipient's name, regiment and number – all useful references for getting into army records. And birth, marriage and death certificates will all indicate other family members, occupations and address – so leading to census returns, maps showing where they lived at the time, and possibly records of occupations – as well as giving evidence of migration and mobility.

A trick with elderly relatives is to make them curious rather than suspicious. So try to show some interest in them as individuals – even though it is their possessions you are hoping

Here's an idea for you… **Make sure you look after your family heirlooms by keeping them out of direct sunlight and store them in a cool place away from any potential danger from damp or insect infestation. Try to avoid handling them too much as well. Make copies of documents if you can. There are lots of excellent 'storage solutions' available. Using the proper materials to store your valuable memorabilia won't be cheap but it will undoubtedly be money well spent and you, and your descendants, won't regret it.**

to see. They need to think they are going to be as interesting to you while they are alive as they will be when they are dead!

Sometimes a 'find' will produce as many questions as it answers so try to get to the bottom of matters as you go along. Birthday books are great because they tell you the date of someone's birthday (but not the year). But if it just says something like '14 May, Maisie' you are not much further forward until you know who Maisie is, or was.

Probably, the most exciting finds are going to be family photographs. For more thoughts on these and what they may really be saying to you, see IDEA 46, *Families in focus*.

Try another idea…

Working with the belongings of members of your family is a very meaningful experience. Talking to those who actually knew those now departed, or have stories to tell about them, is something that can never be replaced by searching the bland lists and indexes to be found in record offices and libraries. But be warned: try to be a little detached as you undertake these investigations or there is the danger that you may be imbued with ideas and thoughts that are a little fanciful.

Every family will be different, but here are a few examples of the things to look out for that may contain some piece of vital information.

Account books • Address books • Awards • Baptism certificates • Birth, marriage and death certificates • Birthday and Christmas cards • Birthday books • Club and society memberships • Deeds • Diaries and journals • Diplomas • Divorce papers • Employment records • Family Bibles • Grave deeds

'Junk is anything that has outlived its usefulness.'
OLIVER HERFORD (1863–1935)
American humorous writer and illustrator

Defining idea…

• Insurance papers • Letters • Medical cards • Military records • Newspaper cuttings • Obituaries • Passports • Pension records • Photographs and portraits • Printed announcements • School prize books • School reports • Scrapbooks • Visitors' books • Wedding books • Wills and other probate documents

How did it go?

Q **My old gran insists that she has nothing of any use or interest to me. Do you think she might be right?**

A *Almost certainly, no. Working on the premise that nothing truly outlives its usefulness, you need to persuade her (politely and gently, of course) that she should let you be the judge of what might be interesting. I wouldn't necessarily advocate poking about under her bed yourself – that voyage of discovery may not be entirely what you wanted.*

Q **I can see me ending up as the family record keeper but my husband is a de-cluttering freak and he won't be too enamoured if I start a collection of boxes full of really interesting old papers. How might I win him over?**

A *Try to get him interested in some particular aspect of your investigations rather than taking on the whole gamut. Often those who are not interested in 'family' are nevertheless interested in the house, place or community they live in now.*

4

Is there anybody out there?

You're not alone – there are countless others trying to discover more about themselves or their communities. Contacting them can only help you with your own researches.

The study of family history is not a recent phenomenon — genealogies are among the very earliest historical narratives. All you need to do is identify who else is investigating in your area of interest.

Finding others who are actively working on the same genealogical lines as you are allows you to tap into a valuable, usually unpublished, research source. Perhaps they have already covered the ground you hope to tread, thus helping you with your research. In addition, there are numerous everyday lists that can aid you in your efforts to discover these folk.

Try looking in telephone directories or at the voting lists for your areas of interest if you're attempting to locate potential unknown relatives. These can be found via the local reference library or, of course, can be accessed on the internet (see www.192.com), although there may be a charge involved.

Here's an idea for you… **Tread carefully with your research and do not take as gospel some lengthy pedigree which apparently enables you to claim an impressively long descent from royalty (or other distinguished person or notorious criminal). It is tempting to accept information as totally true, particularly when you see it on screen or in print, but don't. Instead, take this pedigree as potentially valuable information whose accuracy and reliability you have to check and confirm before you incorporate it into your own family tree. Furthermore, don't continue unless you can verify everything you've already collected.**

Family history societies throughout the world collect and publish the surnames being researched by their members (members' interests) – basically, 'who' is researching 'what' surname and 'where'. These are usually published in book form, on CD, on microfiche or on the society website. Many family and local history magazines, usually published monthly, also contain lists of research interests, offering this service to their readers usually free of charge.

There are also several specialist genealogical directories that are published annually specifically for the purpose of enabling people to make contact with others researching the same names in the same places. These can be purchased as books, CDs or microfiche. Copies of these publications may also be found in your local reference library.

Always check to see if anyone is undertaking a one-name study of any of the names you are interested in. Often the 'one-namer' will be researching all occurrences of a surname, as opposed to a particular pedigree. Although some one-namers may restrict their research geographically, perhaps to one country, many one-namers collect all occurrences found anywhere in the world.

Many commercial family history data providers also have the facility for you to record and submit your own family tree to their websites, allowing you to help create one large worldwide family tree. Conveniently for researchers, these are held in a searchable database to allow easy access and show links to potential relatives. These sites also enable you to create your own profile so that other researchers or family members can find you. Many of these commercial sites also host message boards or run news lists.

So, how do you find out more about the origins and demography of the surnames that you are researching? Get some pointers in IDEA 1, What's in a name?

Try another idea...

The various publicly available online regional (usually county-based) genealogy news lists, chat rooms or message/query boards are other great places to 'bump' into other people researching one of your family lines. They are designed to be a practical resource for today's family historian and they are exceptionally good value for money as, generally, they can all be accessed free of charge.

Online auction houses are another place that you can find genealogical gems. Try typing your name or your ancestor's surname into their search engine and see what comes up. You might be pleasantly surprised.

Other innovations on the internet are the online community websites specialising in finding old school mates, friends or relatives – be they close or very distant – with the of aim of reconnecting relations and generations. Again, free to register and search, but they make a flat-rate charge for you to access contact details.

'It is a very sad thing that nowadays there is so little useless information.'
OSCAR WILDE (1854-1900)

Defining idea...

How did it go?

Q **I tried subscribing to several genealogical mailing lists but found myself swamped with emails. How can I make life more manageable?**

A   *It is worth subscribing slowly to mailing lists – no more than one or two at a time – and be very selective about the lists to which you subscribe. Make sure that you are subscribing to a list that is going to help you progress your research or knowledge. Even within the genealogy community, lists can cover a huge variety of specialities, be it area or regional, ethnic or religious. It might also be better to receive any mail as a daily digest instead of individual emails.*

Q **I am looking into an ancestor called John Smith ... along with thousands of other people! How can I try to locate people researching 'my' John Smith?**

A   *When looking at who is researching a particular name, it is very important to look at where that name is actually being researched – particularly if the name is fairly common, as yours is. If you limit yourself to concentrating on those researching Smiths in the same village or town where your Smiths are, it will quickly help you to determine if it may be someone researching the same line or family as your are. Definitely avoid contacting those people who are just fishing and looking for John Smith 'anywhere'.*

5

Truth and lies

By asking questions, particularly of your older relatives, you could get vital clues about your family's past. However, don't rely completely on family stories before you've cross-checked them with other sources.

For centuries, individuals, families and societies have been researching families, homes, villages and towns. And this may be your family, home, village or town.

It is so important to speak to the older relatives while they are still around, but don't stop there – the younger generations may know more or different snippets. Grandparents often have more time to spend with their grandchildren than they did with their own children, so tales of their childhoods and families may skip a generation. My grandmother had eleven siblings altogether, with four sisters still alive when I first started researching my past. Each sister knew something different and would occasionally disagree about a simple 'fact'. The importance of contacting every known relative is therefore obvious.

It's unlikely that you will know all your living relatives. You may possibly have a name or two for your more distant relatives but not much more. However, it is possible that these are the very family members who will hold the vital clues you will need to progress your investigations into your family's past. Discovering these 'lost' relatives needs to be an important part of your initial investigations.

There is an effective trick you can try when talking to relatives, particularly the older ones – slip into the conversation a deliberate 'falsehood'. This can be especially useful if the old dear is being overly reticent and stubbornly non-cooperative. Mention a totally fictitious event concerning a great-uncle, for example, about whom you really want to know more. You will soon be corrected and more real information can then often be forthcoming. I have sometimes even made up a relative just to get the reaction 'Don't you mean ...?'.

How you approach your relatives depends on several things: How well do you know them? Where do they live? Are they on the internet? Do you personally prefer phoning or writing? The choice is yours, but which method you go for is relatively unimportant, although there is a lot to be said in favour of writing, especially to those you do not know too well, or at all.

You can include a simple questionnaire laying out the problems you would like resolved. These questions can be quite specific, being about names, dates or places, or perhaps a birth or a marriage. You could also ask about what school someone went to, or if they served in the armed forces, or what they did for a living. Other questions can be more general, enquiring about any photographs, a family Bible, letters, stories about the family and so forth. And remember, you can, and should, always go back with further queries;

so don't try to get too much into your initial enquiry or you might put the relative off.

It is important to make sure that the people you are contacting know who you are. If you know very little about them then the chances are they will know little or nothing about you. Explain who you are and try to reassure them from the outset that your research is just for your and the current family's own benefit. Emphasise that you merely want to build a bigger, better and more accurate picture of the family for posterity and that this is not part of some scam to do them out of their inheritance. Many people are, quite understandably, protective of their own history and need to be assured that what you are doing is not going to undermine that.

Accounts from relatives may contradict each other, or be at variance with your own memory. This is not a problem provided you keep a note of where each piece of information came from and you check everything in the records whenever you can.

Don't blindly dismiss those unlikely family stories. There might be claims of descent from a famous person, such as the Duke of Gloucester, but, on investigation, you find that an ancestor ran a pub of that name or was just the potman there. Somewhere there is usually an element of truth, however confused. My great-great-great-grandfather may not have been Mayor of Hungerford, but he certainly lived there.

Be prepared for a whole range of emotions, from frustration to elation, but the bottom line is that it will be incredibly rewarding.

Try another idea…

While you are asking your family about their memories, don't forget to ask what old papers, photographs and the like they may have. Have a look at IDEA 3, *Show and tell*.

Defining idea…

'God gave us our memories so that we may have roses in December.'
JAMES MATTHEW BARRIE (1860–1937) Scottish dramatist and novelist

How did it go?

Q **How can I possibly approach a great-aunt I've never met and expect some constructive help?**

A *One way to unearth the information you are after from distant relatives is to send a copy of the facts that you do already have, perhaps in the form of a simple family tree. Most people can understand these whereas if you constantly just refer to great-grandmother this or second-cousin that, it is easy for them to become confused.*

Q **Everyone I speak to tells me that great-grandfather was born on 24 September 1879, but I can find nothing to confirm this as being so. Why might that be?**

A *Relatives may insist that your forebear was born on that date, but perhaps he in fact was not. The answer is often to look a year or two either side, when you might discover he was actually born on 24 September 1881. Then again, the date of birth may occasionally be found to be exactly a week out, possibly because the registrar misinterpreted 'she was born last Wednesday', or it was a deliberate false statement in order to avoid having to pay a fine for a late registration.*

6

Join the club

Local history societies and family history societies abound in all parts of the world. Their journals and books are a rich source of help and advice if you know how to use them effectively.

You'll need to understand the difference between local and family history societies to be able to get the best from both in your quest for information.

Family history societies promote and assist the study of genealogy and family history. Their prime interest is the study of people and, secondly, the places where those people live. Local history societies concentrate on an actual physical place or area and are, therefore, interested in the people because of where they live.

Family historians need to be able to set their ancestors in the context of the society or place where they lived – and thus depend on the work and expertise of the local historian. The two disciplines rely on many of the same sources, but apply them using different methods. Family historians need an understanding of the ways in which local historians use records, particularly unusual or unique sources that local historians may have identified. Reading local histories of the communities where your ancestors lived can help you to build on the information that you already have.

Conversely, local historians need the work genealogists do in transcribing sources such as parish registers and monumental inscriptions. They also need their support in lobbying for improved access to libraries and archives. The writing of family history easily merges into the writing of local history.

Local history enriches our lives, both as individuals and as whole communities. It is an area where amateur and professional can meet and work profitably together. Local historians range from interested individuals and members of local societies to professional archivists in the field and university lecturers. There are many thousands of people now actively involved in making a valuable contribution towards enriching and extending our understanding of the past.

Each county in the British Isles has its own family history society or societies. Within each county there may be local societies covering a town or city and its surrounding area. Most

Here's an idea for you… **Join a society in the area that you live, even if your genealogical interests are in a different region. By attending their meetings, not only will you meet a lot of like-minded people but you will also find out what research resources are available to you locally.**

towns have a local history society while most villages either have a society or individuals who are extremely knowledgeable about the area and its history.

To see who else might be researching or interested in your family, village or town, look at IDEA 4, *Is there anybody out there?*

Try another idea…

SO, HOW CAN SOCIETIES HELP YOU WITH YOUR RESEARCH?

Most societies produce a quarterly journal containing historical articles about life in the area, general articles describing local records, information about local indexes and what's new or going on in the area. These journals also list members' interests (who is researching a specific surname in a specific area, for instance), helping members to contact others who share their research interests.

Societies hold regular meetings, often centred around a lecture, typically with an expert speaker. More importantly for our purposes here, these meetings give attendees the opportunity to obtain assistance and advice and meet others with similar interests, all on a mutual self-help basis. A bookstall is generally available at these meetings, giving the opportunity to peruse the latest book titles. Societies are run by volunteers so they do not usually have the resources to undertake research on your behalf; but they are able to offer guidance on your own research. Some societies also organise day schools, conferences and courses that aim at extending your level of expertise as well as being interesting and entertaining. Many organise trips to The

'There is not a sprig of grass that shoots uninteresting to me.'
THOMAS JEFFERSON (1743–1826)

Defining idea…

National Archives and other record repositories. Some societies also have research rooms containing various general family history sources, transcribed records, indexes and sometimes historical material relating to their area of interest. Admission to these research rooms is generally free for members.

Family and local history societies have, for a number of years, been transcribing and indexing local records, such as census returns, parish registers, monumental inscriptions, Poor Law records, apprenticeship indentures, settlement examinations, land tax assessments and Quarter Sessions order books. Much of this work has been published in various formats including book, microfiche, CD and it is available to purchase or view on the internet. Alternatively, these indexes can usually be searched for a small fee by contacting the society.

Q   **Are there any special interest family history societies?**

How did it go?

A   *Yes, there are societies covering specialist areas of research such as Anglo-Germans, Anglo-Italians, Catholics, Families in British India, Jewish families, Quakers, Railway Ancestors and a Romany and Traveller Family History Society. There is also another specialist type of 'society' – a one-name study. A one-name study is a project researching all occurrences of a specific surname. These may concentrate on aspects such as geographi-cal distribution of the name and the changes in that distribution over the centuries, or may attempt to reconstruct the genealogy of as many lines as possible bearing the name. One-namers often make an attempt to quantify the rarity of their name. A co-operative effort between people studying the same surname bears much fruit and the people involved have a good chance of discovering new relatives, depending of course on how common the name is.*

Q   **How do you locate the contact details of a society?**

A   *Your local archive, record office or local studies library should have a list of societies and the history experts based in your area. They should also be able to inform you of specialist publications that give societies' full contact details. Check, too, if the society in your area of interest has a website.*

7

Hatches, matches and despatches

Since the mid-nineteenth century, the government has been officially recording births, marriages and deaths. Join us to glean the most from these records.

The cause of death given on a 1927 death certificate: 'Syncope due to double bronchopneumonia consequent upon toxaemia due to burns of buttocks, legs and arms caused by ignition of clothes by lighted candle in searching for bed bugs. Verdict: Misadventure.'

The demand for parliamentary reform went back to the mid-1700s. No account had been made of the dramatic changes in the British way of life due to the Industrial Revolution. This eventually resulted, during the 1830s, in a number of significant

Here's an idea for you... **If your direct ancestor was born before civil registration commenced in 1837 or you are unable to locate their birth in the indexes, try to locate the birth certificate of a sibling, which will give you the same information that you require to advance your research.**

reforms. One of these was the extremely important compulsory registration of births, marriages and deaths (1836), which came into force on 1 July 1837. Without this system of civil registration, it would have been impossible to enforce the Factory Acts, which sought to protect children and young people, who could now rely on their birth certificates to prove their age. The reforms also provided valuable statistical information.

Civil registration records have proved to be a treasure trove of information for family and local historians, helping to verify events and also fill in the gaps in our family trees. Even as we go through our own lives, we increasingly need certified copies of our own birth certificates to prove who we are or who we are married to. When we die we cannot be buried or cremated without having a death certificate.

The basic information provided varies. Birth certificates give the date and place where the event occurred, the child's forename(s), and the name and occupation of the father, the name and maiden surname of the mother (with her usual residence if the birth took place elsewhere), and the name and address of the informant for the registration. A marriage certificate gives the names and usually the ages of the marrying couple, their addresses and occupations, the names and occupations of their fathers, the date and place of marriage, and the names of the witnesses. Death certificates record name, date, place, age, cause of death, occupation, residence if different from the place of death, and the name and address of the informant for registration. A slight word of caution: because the quarterly indexes are based on the date the event was registered and not the date of the actual event, you should remember that if you are searching for an ancestor who was born on 21 December 1921 the birth may not have been registered until January – meaning that the record would be found in the 'March 1922' quarter rather than the 'December 1921' index as you may assume.

A search of the national death indexes after 1866 will give you a person's age on death, or date of birth from 1969. This can provide you with just the information you need to help you locate your ancestors on the census. See IDEA 13, *The sense of the census*.

Try another idea...

More importantly, apart from giving you the basic information that helps you to go back another generation, the information given on birth, death and marriage certificates taken together also provides valuable detail that can open up lots more avenues for your research.

The recorded cause of death given above from 1927, for example, can lead you to local newspaper reports of the actual accident, obituaries, funeral and floral tributes. The words 'Verdict: Misadventure' suggest there was a coroner's inquest, another valuable source of information, which again may have been reported in the local newspapers.

'It is a mistake to try to look too far ahead. The chain of destiny can only be grasped one link at a time.'
WINSTON CHURCHILL (1874–1965)

Defining idea...

How did it go?

Q From the civil registration death indexes, I have the date of birth of my ancestor, who died in 1970. But why can't I find the relevant entry for his birth?

A   *If, despite having the exact date of birth, you cannot find the entry that you are looking for, and you've checked the quarters immediately before and after that date, then you need to treat the information with some caution and broaden your search, working forward from the last known 'sighting' of your ancestor. People often remember the birthday of relatives but not necessarily a year of birth or age. Your ancestor may have been one of the many who for various reasons changed their age. Make sure that you also check the 'male' and 'female' entries – found at the end of each surname – just in case the parents were unable to decide on a forename for the baby. Another possibility is, of course, that your ancestor was not born in England or Wales, although similar systems do operate in Scotland and Ireland.*

Q Why can't I find my ancestor in the indexes?

A   *The most common reason why you can't locate your ancestor is that the basic information you have is incorrect. How reliable is the information that you actually have? Just because it is in writing does not mean that the details are correct. Remember: any information is only as good as the person who gave it. My parents' marriage certificate contains several inaccuracies – information provided by my father. My father's name on the certificate is not the same as that on his birth certificate. It also states his father was deceased, which he wasn't – he died ten years after my parents married.*

8

Let no man put asunder

Not as common as it is now, but the best of intentions have often ended in separation and divorce in the past. And if not the latter, then wife-selling or bigamy may have resulted.

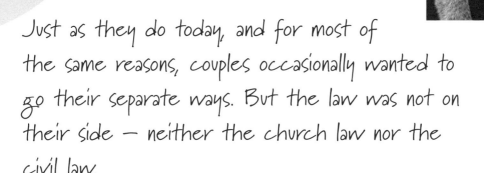

Just as they do today, and for most of the same reasons, couples occasionally wanted to go their separate ways. But the law was not on their side — neither the church law nor the civil law.

In 2004, 167,116 divorces were granted in the UK, the highest number since 1996, and the fourth successive annual increase. Around 70% of divorces were granted to the wife, the most frequent grounds for which being the unreasonable behaviour of her husband. For a man, it was separation for two years with consent. The highest number of divorces in the UK was recorded in 1993 at 180,018.

By the beginning of the seventeenth century, England and Wales were the only Protestant countries in Europe not to have some form of divorce, which, at least, allowed the innocent party to remarry. The church did provide for a divorce *a mensa et thoro* (from bed and board), which allowed a separation on the grounds of life-threatening

Here's an idea for you...

Discovering that there was a divorce, or more likely just a separation, in the family can be quite difficult as it is the sort of thing people don't tell the grandchildren, so tread carefully. This is an area where you need to be sure of your facts and you may have to be quite persistent when speaking to those older, living relatives. Look carefully at the census returns to see if there is a change of name, particularly for the 'wife' for whom you cannot find any marriage to the 'husband'.

cruelty or adultery, but no remarriage while one of the couple lived; or a divorce *a vicula matrimonii* (from the chain of marriage), which declared a marriage invalid, and allowed remarriage, because of non-consummation within two years, or impotence, frigidity, lunacy, incest, bigamy and some other reasons.

During the late-seventeenth century, a process evolved for obtaining divorce by an Act of Parliament. This was inordinately expensive and by 1857 there had been less than four hundred such cases. By the eighteenth century, it was generally assumed that if one of a married couple disappeared for seven years the other became free to remarry. However, if the errant partner returned then the first marriage took precedence. Under common law, deserted wives became a charge on the parish, as did any children. The husbands would be pursued and brought before the magistrates (in much the same way that absent fathers are brought to account by the Child Support Agency today).

Everything was to change in 1858 following the Divorce and Matrimonial Causes Act, which abolished the authority of the church courts. The new London-based Court for Divorce and Matrimonial Causes now heard all divorce and matrimonial cases. A husband could obtain a divorce for adultery. A wife had to prove adultery plus another offence: desertion for two years or more, bigamy, incest, cruelty, rape or unnatural offences.

The Matrimonial Causes Act 1937 extended the grounds for divorce in England and Wales to adultery, cruelty, desertion for three years, refusal to consummate, insanity, epilepsy or venereal disease in a communicable form at the time of marriage. The 1969 Divorce Reform Act made irretrievable breakdown of a marriage the sole grounds.

Since adultery did not constitute grounds for divorce until after 1858, a husband would have no legal sanction over his wife's extramarital liaisons, which might well have resulted in his having to raise another man's child – or even children – under his own roof. As divorce, and consequently the freedom to remarry legally, was hardly ever an option for the ordinary working man or woman before the twentieth century, desertion and bigamy were not uncommon. Some self-respect might have been recovered if the man could, at least, dispose of his wife by selling her at a public auction. The buyer was usually the 'paramour' and the whole business was usually prearranged. Records of such sales are rare, although a newspaper report or Deed of Sale might occasionally come to light.

With partner-changing being far more prevalent than most people would have expected, the legitimacy of the children can sometimes be in doubt. Can genetic research help? See IDEA 36, *Helical help.*

Try another idea…

'Divorce is like matrimony: a fellow has to go through it three or four times before he knows how.'
EDGAR SALTUS (1855–1921)
American author

Defining idea…

'My first wife divorced me on the grounds of incompatibility, and besides, I think she hated me.'
OSCAR LEVANT (1906–1972)
American pianist, composer and wit

Defining idea…

How did it go?

Q   I can't find any evidence that my several times great-grand-mother ever married her second 'husband' and I know her first husband died after her. Yet she lived with this other man, took his surname and had several children by him. Could this happen if she was not properly divorced from husband number one?

A   Not only could it happen, but it very often did. There were only about forty divorces each year in the 1840s but the number of married individuals who moved in with another would have been hugely in excess of this.

Q   I know that a couple of my ancestors divorced in the twentieth century. Will I be able to find the reasons because I'd really like to discover a bit of scandal in the family?

A   Files covering all matrimonial cases from 1858, which started in London, are held at The National Archives. However, since 1927, only samples have been kept. Files from the District Registries are all destroyed after 25 years – only that for Wallis Simpson in 1936 survives – the decrees only being retained. The Divorce Registry in London has composite indexes to all decrees absolute issued in England and Wales from 1858, no matter where they were granted.

9

All the news that's fit to print

Newspapers are a fantastic resource for the local and family historian. They are full of information – both about people and places – that you will rarely find recorded anywhere else.

From the early seventeenth century, newspapers have been recording the news, both local and national. With obituaries, scandal, announcements, advertisements, sales particulars and so forth, they were little different to those we know today.

Newsletters were flourishing in England by the 1560s. Although the first printing press had arrived in 1477, it was another hundred years before type replaced hand

If you have found something in a newspaper relating to an ancestor, don't stop there. Think about what follow-up stories or other records will have been generated by that event and search them out.

written copies. It was during the reign of James I that printing really began to take its place in distributing the news, with enterprising writers and printers producing pamphlets describing events and manipulating public opinion with editorial comment. The English Civil War saw an increase in the reporting of domestic news. This was followed during the 1660s by the introduction of coffee houses, whose customers further fuelled the thirst for news. People also became increasingly aware of the relationship between the written word, power and politics.

By 1643, London had about twelve weekly titles. The first provincial newspapers appeared around 1701, although they tended to concentrate mainly on national and international news. The development of freedom of speech also rapidly followed. However, it wasn't until 1855 that tax on 'print and knowledge' was finally abolished.

Newspapers fall into four main categories. (1) The broadsheets, which, as today, consisted of large sheets of paper. Old broadsheets are very rare. They were originally printed just on one side so they could be posted on billboards and were never intended to survive. (2) Local or provincial newspapers. (3) National magazines: established in the early 1800s, these were either weekly or monthly publications, with articles covering general news, travel accounts, etc. (4) Specialist magazines devoted to various topics, just as there are today.

Most newspapers traditionally carried announcements for births, marriages and deaths; plus, in more recent times, forthcoming marriages, accounts of weddings, anniversaries, birthdays and 'in memoriams'. The associated obituaries and accounts of funerals can often give a person's entire life history. Newspapers must, therefore, be one of the best genealogical sources available. However, like any secondary sources, the information found within really does need to be confirmed using any primary sources that are available to you.

Did your ancestor die as the result of an accident or was the death the subject of an inquest? If so, then undoubtedly the local newspaper will have reported on it. The more horrendous the details, the more you are likely to find it in print. Since the earliest times newspapers have thrived on the tragedies, tribulations and misfortunes of not only the great but also everyday folk as well. After all, that is what really sells the papers – it is important to remember that newspaper proprietors moulded the content and style of their publications to appeal to their readership.

You could fully explore the myths and facts of some of those family stories by locating related newspaper items. Begin by looking at IDEA 2, *Who told you that?*

Try another idea...

'*Were it left to me to decide whether we should have a government without newspapers, or newspapers without a government, I should not hesitate a moment to prefer the latter.*'
THOMAS JEFFERSON (1743–1826)

Defining idea...

In the past, especially in the nineteenth century, the press carried very detailed reports of local governing bodies, such as the School Board and Local Board of Health. You will also find property sales (land and houses), legal notices and advertisements of all kinds, providing an essential source of history written as it was happening.

Newspapers also played an important role in the emigration process, with the notices they carried providing information about the means of emigrating; information about the departure and arrival of ships; and the publication in advertisements of the names of local agents through whom passages might be arranged. Ships' notices also carried details of the availability of parcels of land that were on offer to prospective immigrants.

You might think that your ancestors were probably quite lowly and achieved very little, but are you really, really sure? For the local and family historian all news has to be good news.

Q **How can I get the best out of using newspapers?**

How did it go?

A *Unless you know the date of a specific event, searching newspapers can be very difficult. However, the national papers can provide priceless information about what was going on in the world at the time your ancestors lived, while local newspapers can tell you what was happening in the community. They can paint a detailed picture of the life and times of your ancestors in a way few other sources really can. Several commercial companies are now digitising old newspapers and are in the process making them fully searchable. Indexes do exist for several national newspapers and are usually available in major libraries. There is also a Periodical Source Index, a subject index covering genealogy and local history periodicals. Coverage starts from about 1800. However, individual names that are mentioned in passing will not appear in the index.*

Q **Where do I find copies of historical newspapers?**

A *The major collection of national and local newspapers and periodicals in the United Kingdom can be found as part of the British Library's newspaper collection in London. Your local reference library should possess copies of any surviving local newspapers. Using the internet, you should also be able to locate historical newspaper images, containing pictures from some of the most interesting events in more recent history. There are also a number of publications that list what is available and where. Facsimile copies of historical newspapers for specific dates are also available to purchase.*

10

Did he fall or was he pushed?

Our most intriguing ancestors are dead ones, particularly if their end was of the sticky variety. Coroners' records and newspapers may reveal all.

The notion that our ancestors all died peacefully in their beds is, thankfully, a fallacy. Coming a close second to the miscreant ancestor in the popularity stakes is the one whose death was unusual — the more unusual the better.

If it isn't a family story passed down through the generations, then the first discovery that something untoward may have happened to an ancestor is often made when looking at the ordinary recording of his or her death. Death certificates,

Here's an idea for you… **Have another look at any death certificates you may have and see if in the 'Informant' box there is any reference to the coroner or a coroner's inquest. From 1837, a registrar could not record a sudden, suspicious or industrial death without the coroner being involved. He could insist on a post-mortem examination and, in any case, provided the certificate for the body to be released and the death to be registered. Unless the death was really of major importance, it is probably only the local newspapers that would have covered the events, so concentrate on discovering where these are now held and seeing if they have got the details you hope they have.**

issued from the mid-nineteenth century, have always given the cause of death – although too often it is something totally benign such as 'Visitation of God' or 'Old Age'. Far more gripping would be: Thomas Stevens died in 1891, 'Accidentally killed by the fall of large mass from a stack of manure' – his last words can only be guessed at. And, in 1939, while enjoying a quiet walk along Beachy Head in Sussex, Mary Florence Savory died from 'Crushing of the skull & evisceration of the brain due to being struck by the air screw of an aeroplane after its crashing to earth'.

Parish burial registers though do not normally give such detailed, if any, information, except perhaps where the death was exceptional. 'Teeth' is a not an uncommonly given cause of death. However, don't get too excited about this because it is usually some form of infection or septicaemia resulting from teething – nothing to do with a bite from a mad dog.

From the late twelfth century, county coroners were appointed to enquire into mysterious and unexpected deaths. Originally their job was to collect evidence, conduct an inquest and then make a judgement on any sudden death, death in abnormal or suspicious circumstances, and deaths in prisons and lunatic asylums. Suicides, homicides, deaths by misadventure from famine or plague, fatal accidents, drowning, and death by fire all came under the coroners' jurisdiction, resulting in the inevitable paperwork any bureaucracy produces.

Most deaths are going to be natural or accidental, but others may have involved a perpetrator who was subsequently brought to justice. See IDEA 33, *Crime and punishment*.

Try another idea…

In most cases, a jury helped the coroner draw his conclusions and in the early days could even nominate suspected felons. Coroners' inquests have always taken place in public – in earlier centuries, frequently in the local public house with everyone sitting around the corpse. The press were of course not excluded and since the publication of newspapers and periodicals, accounts have appeared in both local and national media.

You may find coroners' records, including bills, accounts, expense claims (vouchers) and post-mortem reports, in county archives. However, it is the witness statements

'Don't go into Mr McGregor's garden. Your Father had an accident there: he was put in a pie by Mrs McGregor.'
From *The Tale of Peter Rabbit* by
BEATRIX POTTER (1866–1943)

Defining idea…

'Murder, like talent, seems occasionally to run in families.'
GEORGE HENRY LEWIS (1817–1878)
English writer

(depositions) that are often the most rewarding and get to the crux of what really happened. When George Edward Duckett died after a fall from a window while working at 4 Harcourt Buildings, Temple in London on 23 August 1850, there was obviously concern that someone may have 'done for 'im'. An inquest was called, the same day, in the Plough Inn 'on view of the body of George Edward Duckett now here lying dead'. Having heard evidence from the son that his father had been in good health and not 'suffered any swimming of the head', and from a fellow workman that there was no one else around at the time of the fall, a verdict of Accidental Death was pronounced.

Q   **I'm supposed to have a great-grandfather who committed suicide by drowning himself in the local river. Are there records of
those as well?**

*How did
it go?*

A   *The verdict from a coroner's inquest may be suicide or 'deceased took
his own life while of unsound mind'. Before 1961, when suicide was not
only taboo but also illegal (self murder as it was sometimes known), many
courts would have opted for the less condemnatory verdict or simply left
it as 'open'. So, when Elizabeth Adams drowned herself and her infant
daughter in a stream in Edmonton, Middlesex in 1841, their death certificates both just give 'drowned' as the cause of death although the mother's
postnatal depression, almost certainly undiagnosed then, was probably the
true cause.*

Q   **My mother says her great-uncle was killed in 'mysterious circumstances' during the early 1900s but I can't find any specific
records about it. Why might that be?**

A   *Records of coroners' inquests tend to be very good – but, sadly, only until
1875. The 1958 Public Records Act introduced some regrettable decisions
regarding coroners' records. Essentially, all records pre-1875 had to be preserved, together with those relating to treasure trove or 'matters of special
historical interest', but those after that date were to be handled quite
differently, resulting in the majority henceforth being destroyed after 15
years. It is therefore for the years after 1875 that newspapers really come
into their own, and they are often the only source of detailed information
that can flesh out the often bland and enigmatic entry on a death certificate or in a burial register.*

11

Writ in stone

Slabs, brasses, headstones, memorial gardens, crematoria and churchyards can all bring the dead back to life for you – metaphorically speaking, that is.

'Here lies the remains of James Paddy, brickmaker, late of this parish, in the hope that his clay will be re-moulded in a workmanlike manner far superior to his former perishable materials.'

'Monumental inscription' is a term used for anything that is engraved or written on any type of memorial, from gravestones in a graveyard to massive monuments. These are an invaluable source of information for family and local historians alike, as in the example above – be it not as complimentary as it could be.

The earliest inscribed memorials are found within the churches themselves, installed in the sixteenth century by the wealthier inhabitants of the parish. These memorials can take the form of effigies, monuments, memorial brasses, windows, benefactors' boards, vases, pews, organs, lecterns or communion plates, all of which may have inscriptions. In the churchyard, graves were originally either unmarked or occasionally marked with a wooden cross or grave-board which soon rotted away.

The seventeenth century saw the better-off marking their place of burial with gravestones. Unfortunately churchyards were often cleared as they filled up, the bones being removed to a charnel house and the ground reused for new interments. What gravestones there were did not always survive.

Monumental inscriptions can contain all sorts of information. As well as the date and cause of death and occasionally date of birth, they can also outline relationships and give an occupation (either as text or emblems, such as tools of the trade used by the deceased). In addition, monumental inscriptions can carry a hidden message (although occasionally it is forthright, as in the James Paddy example!). Evidence of migration or immigration may also be revealed.

Although comparatively few families were armigerous, a coat-of-arms on a memorial can help distinguish the family from others of the same name. The College of Arms was responsible for the supervision of the funerals of armigers, as well as the use of arms and epitaphs on monuments, and also issued funeral certificates. These are a rich source of family information and can describe not only the deceased but also provide information on the extended family.

With luck you can easily construct a substantial family tree from a single monument. Finding a mother, father and children buried together and all appearing on the gravestone is not unusual. Even the simplest inscription can fill a gap in your family tree and help prove the relationship between two individuals. It not common to find several family graves grouped together in a churchyard. Many nonconformists didn't keep burial registers for their burial grounds, especially Catholics. Monumental inscriptions can therefore be a vital record for researching nonconformist ancestors.

Here's an idea for you... **Include photographs of your families' gravestones in your family history file. It will create interest and may be the only 'visible presence' your ancestor has.**

The building of the great Victorian cemeteries helped to alleviate the problems of disease caused by overcrowded churchyards. The movement in favour of cremation was based on similar concerns, the first official cremation taking place in 1885.

Memorials to those cremated may be found in the garden of remembrance or elsewhere nearby. These can take the form of plaques on walls or kerbstones, or on plaques dedicating rose bushes, trees, benches etc. Ashes may, with permission, be buried in the consecrated ground of a churchyard. In this case there should not only be an entry in the parish burial register, but possibly also a monumental inscription in the churchyard itself.

The only permanent record at the crematorium is an entry in the Book of Remembrance. These, unlike the Cremation Registers (equivalent to Burial Registers), are available for inspection and can sometimes include information in addition to name and date of death, such as age, date of birth and any official position held.

For centuries, antiquaries and historians have used monumental inscriptions to prepare their histories, and thus also transcribed and recorded them, resulting in the survival of transcriptions of monumental inscriptions from graveyards that 'disappeared' long ago. More recently this has been undertaken by family history societies. Most of these have been published and may be

Try another idea...

Just because a name appears on a gravestone does not mean that that person was buried there. Check the burial register to confirm who is actually buried there. This is especially important with memorials within churches, which often refer to those buried elsewhere. See IDEA 22, *Open the doors and see the people*.

Defining idea...

'If a man needs an elaborate tombstone in order to remain in the memory of his country, it is clear that his living at all was an act of absolute superfluity.'
OSCAR WILDE (1854–1900)

49

available for purchase. Otherwise, copies can be found deposited at the local archives. If you are really lucky, you may find something on the internet.

How did it go?

Q **I've been extremely fortunate in discovering what appears to be a very early and detailed family gravestone. However, its condition looks too good to be true. Should I trust it?**

A *You are right to be suspicious. Tombstones with what appear to be very early dates should be treated with caution because information was often inscribed retrospectively – that is, a stone erected for one generation could have details of the parents included at the same time. Hence, the ages and dates are very possibly inaccurate. Careful examination of the inscription may reveal that a number of burials were recorded only when the most recent burial occurred, the giveaway being that all of the inscription itself has obviously been cut at the same time.*

Q **I have discovered that an ancestor was buried in a large grave-yard. Unfortunately the stone has gone and the monumental inscriptions have not been recorded. How can I discover exactly where my ancestor was laid to rest and if there is any surviving information?**

A *It's not as difficult as you might think. There will almost certainly be a plan of the graveyard or churchyard and/or interments register, both of which will have references to grave numbers. Often these can be found either with the local vicar or church warden, or deposited at the local county record office/archive.*

12

Reading, 'riting, 'rithmetic

The provision of free education for all was part of the push for social reform and improvement of the masses. Now it also provides history hunters with a new source of information.

Education records are an excellent and often overlooked source of family and local history. Not only can they give you information about a child's formative years, but also factual information about the whole family and the community in which they were placed.

Some of the earliest schools were public schools, founded by local eminent businessmen. Despite them being 'public', they were only open to those with sufficient funds to pay the fees. During the 1500s, King Henry VIII and his son Edward VI sold off many monasteries and used the revenue to build schools. Several London merchant companies similarly founded schools, many surviving as grammar and independent schools to this day.

These early schools were, of course, beyond the reach of the mass of the people, who were lucky to receive a few years of basic education in what were known as voluntary schools. The voluntary schools included Sunday schools, which were first established in 1763, and Dame schools, which were small private schools run by elderly women from their homes (little more than child-minding establishments). Ragged schools were first opened in 1810 and aimed at the very poor. Lessons were given in whatever accommodation was available and the children were given a basic education and help with finding work. The best-organised of the voluntary schools were those run by the Church of England and nonconformist churches, either in an attempt to improve the lot of the uneducated or as a means of converting 'lost souls'. Hence, they opened both charity and fee-paying schools. The Army and Royal Navy also became involved in education, with the training of soldiers and sailors and other associated personnel. They also established several schools just to educate the children of servicemen.

It wasn't until 1833 that government money, in the form of grants, was given to the Anglican and nonconformist societies for the building of schools for the education of children from poor families. This was steadily increased over the following few years and in the 1840s teacher training colleges and a pupil teacher scheme were established. By the time of the Newcastle Commission Report (1861), although one in seven of the population was thought to be receiving some education, the majority of people were still unable to write a letter or read a newspaper. This resulted in a 'payment by results' scheme being introduced in 1862, with school inspectors testing pupils' reading, writing and arithmetic skills. As is the case today, this system attracted a lot of criticism. Things dramatically changed when Gladstone's reforming Liberal Government

Here's an idea for you...

Many schools were established during the Victorian drive to educate the masses and have long since celebrated their centenaries. Have a look in the local reference library or archives to see if a history has been written about the schools that you are interested in.

decided that it was up to the state to ensure that every child received some education. Forster's Education Act of 1870 divided England into areas and arranged that schools should be set up where provision was insufficient. Legislation in 1876 laid down the principle that all children should receive elementary education, but it was not until 1880 that school attendance became compulsory up to the age of 10. From 1893, compulsory education was extended to age 11, and then raised to age 12 (except for those employed in agriculture) in 1899. There was no further extension until 1918, when the school leaving age was raised to 14, then to 15 in 1947, and finally to age 16 in 1965.

To see a school through the eyes of its earlier scholars, explore IDEA 48, *A rue with a view.* See if you can discover any contemporary postcards of it.

Try another idea…

A variety of records have been generated and are available to consult, including the following.

- Admission registers. Dating from 1870, these give the name, date of birth, date of admission, father's name, address and occupation, and details of previous schools attended.
- Log books. Kept from the 1840s, these deal with general information (e.g. the appointment of teaching staff, punishment records and accounts).
- Withdrawal or discharge registers. These give information on the date a child may have withdrawn from the school and the cause of leaving (e.g. evacuation during the Second World War).
- Local Education Authority records, which contain governors' meetings minutes, committee minutes, lists of school managers and accounts details.

'Education is a wonderful thing, provided you always remember that nothing worth knowing can ever be taught.'
OSCAR WILDE (1854-1900)

Defining idea…

How did it go?

Q   Why did it take until 1880 for schooling to become compulsory?

A   There was a strong belief in earlier times that education of the working classes was unnecessary. They only needed skills for the job for which they were destined; and also, if children spent time in school, a source of cheap labour would be lost. Others thought that educating the masses would lead to increases in vice and crime and also render them insolent to their superiors.

Q   Where will I find school records?

A   Information on schools and their records can be found in a variety of places, including local, charitable and industrial archives, Local Education Authorities, libraries, The National Archives and also the schools themselves. Census records will give information on staff and children at residential schools. Records for workhouse schools may be found amongst Poor Law records. Dame Schools should be found listed in trade and commercial directories as 'private academies', which will also help in finding an address and head of a school or institution. Records from corrective institutions, such as training ships and farm schools, may be found among Quarter Sessions records. Local libraries or the British Library's newspaper collection in London may have back copies of newspapers with stories about a school. The old registers of most of the Public Schools have been published. They can contain valuable genealogical information, and even details of what subsequently happened to the pupils.

13

The sense of the census

One of the most important – and easily accessible – primary resources for local and family historians is the census. Learning how to interpret it properly will pay handsome dividends.

The census records offer a snapshot in time of a particular dwelling on a given night, providing details of a specific family, including servants, lodgers, and visitors.

In the 1881 census of Elland, Yorkshire, Mary Thornton – who is shown as unmarried, aged 52 and born in Elland – is described as the concubine of the head of the household, William Jackson! Census records can be used not only to further your search for ancestors, but also to broaden your knowledge of the wider family or your community, supplementing information found in other sources. Geographic mobility can be easily tracked through the given birthplaces, and social mobility through addresses and occupations.

THE ORIGINS

To help you achieve your goals it is extremely important to remember why these records were generated – which was not for any of us to research our family or local

Look in your county or local archive to see if any of the earlier census returns covering 1801, 1811, 1821 or 1831 have survived for your areas of interest. Although the information that they contain is very basic, where they are available these returns can give you information on people born over 250 years ago.

history. Prior to the eighteenth century, Bishops were responsible for counting the number of families in their diocese, but England was reluctant to adopt a regular official census. By 1798, however, the mood was changing: Thomas Malthus published an essay suggesting that population growth would soon be outstripping supplies of food and other resources, 'Causing Britain to be hit by disease, famine and other disasters'. Frightened by this alarmist view of the future, in a time of bad harvests and food shortages, and driven by the need to know how many men were available to fight the French, Parliament passed 'An Act for taking an Account of the Population' in 1800. The first official census in Britain was taken in 1801. Information was collected from every household by the Overseers of the Poor. This first official headcount revealed the population of Britain (which at that time consisted of the whole of England, Ireland, Scotland and Wales) to be 9 million. By the time of the 1901 census, the population of Britain was estimated to be 37 million.

THE PROCESS

Census enumerators were assigned a specific area and distributed a schedule to every household in that area before the census night. They collected them the day following the census, checked the details and copied them into an enumerator's book. The book and the schedules were then returned to the local registrar who in turn checked them and sent them to the Census Office in London. The information that we see today derives from the enumerators' transcript books, not the original schedules, which were destroyed. Technology did not reach the census until 1911, when punch cards and mechanical sorting were introduced, followed in 1961 by computers.

Since 1801 there has been a census every ten years, except for 1941, during the Second World War. Although the basic methods and principles remain unchanged, new questions have been added as others have been removed. The 1841 census is regarded as the first modern census, when the first Registrar General was made responsible for organising the count. This is the earliest census that has survived in its entirety.

To preserve all individuals' confidentiality, there is a 100-year closure on each census before the general public are allowed access. Thus the official release of the 1911 census won't take place until January 2012.

FACTS GIVEN

The information given in each census will vary slightly but, generally speaking, from 1851 each should contain the following: house address and whether or not the house was inhabited; name of each person that had spent the night in that household and their relationship to the head of the household; each person's marital status; age at last birthday; occupation and place of birth; whether they were an employer or employee or neither; and whether they had any handicap, such as being deaf, dumb, blind, or lunatic.

Try another idea...

Use clues from the census to find birth, marriage, and death records, giving you more personal information and opening up other avenues for research. See IDEA 7, *Hatches, matches and despatches*.

Defining idea...

'The true test of a civilisation is not the census, nor the size of the cities, nor the crops – no, but the kind of man the country turns out.'
RALPH WALDO EMERSON (1803–1882) poet and essayist

How did it go?

Q   Why can't I find my ancestor on the census?

A   *If you are searching online using one of the fantastic indexes with links to the actual census images, it may be that the entry you are looking for has been incorrectly indexed or transcribed, or the name misspelled by the enumerator. If you think this is the case, be creative in your searches and try all spelling variations. Additionally, your ancestor may not have been present in the household on census night, and so might have been enumerated elsewhere or may have been missed by the enumerator. Also, a few census returns have not survived. If after a thorough search using the internet you still can't find them and you know roughly where they lived, it may be worth doing an area search either online or by using microfilm or microfiche copies of the actual returns.*

Q   I've checked the 1901 and 1891 census for my ancestors but a different place of birth is given in each. How can that be?

A   *It's very important to check and record the details given on every census for your ancestors. Places of birth may vary slightly due to boundary changes, places being renamed or because your ancestors did not know exactly where they were born or they were more specific in one census than in another. Generally speaking, the nearer the person was living to their place of birth, the more precise the entry is likely to be. Sadly for those of Irish or Scottish decent, the place of birth is mostly just going to be given as Ireland or Scotland – although you might be lucky enough to find a specific place.*

14

Location, location, location

Just as now, in previous centuries anyone wanting to know the location of a local plumber or undertaker, or even the address of an acquaintance, would turn to a local directory. You can turn those same pages.

In the pages of these now historic volumes are to be found the names and addresses of the tradesmen and residents of yesteryear — your family and forebears or the life-blood of the community in which you now reside.

In Britain, the first recognisable directories made their appearance towards the end of the seventeenth century and were chiefly concerned with listing traders and merchants. Although the idea of directories developed over the following decades, it was not until the early nineteenth century that they really began to come into their own. James Pigot, a Manchester engraver, produced his first provincial directory in 1814. In 1839, Pigot formed a partnership with Isaac Slater. Most of the Pigot and Slater directories were in the form of classified lists of trades, with the information being collected by personal canvass. The *London Post Office Directory*,

Here's an idea for you...

Although directories do have their limitations, they can give considerable information about a place and can be used as a starting point for research, or as a cross-link to other sources, such as the census or rates books. Find a local directory for the place in which you now live and, for any particular year, build up a picture of the community or even just a few streets. Follow through from year to year, and you can trace the development of one area, or one street, from its first appearance, showing changes in use of any one building or premises over the years. Try checking the history of your house, beginning with its first appearance in the streets section and then the names of previous occupants can tracked year by year.

initially called the *New Annual Directory*, was first published in 1800. In 1835, the copyright was sold to Isaac Kelly and, from around 1845, he moved into producing provincial directories as well as those for London. Kelly's was by far the largest, but not the only, publisher to operate during the late nineteenth century and in the years up to 1950. In 1885, Kelly's introduced its London suburban directories, or 'Buff Books'.

From the mid-nineteenth century, urban directories were often divided into four sections: 'streets', listed by street name; 'commercial', listing tradesmen by name; 'trades', listing tradesmen by trade; and 'court', which listed private residents and professionals,

the social class As and Bs of their time. Those directories that were less detailed as far as residents and trades were concerned, because they covered quite large areas (a whole or several counties), frequently include a potted history and a then-current description of the towns and villages covered. These can be a very useful introduction to any new place in your researches.

Directories are not the only place where you can find lists of residents in a particular place. See IDEA 16, *Votes and voters* to learn about electoral registers.

Try another idea…

The ever-increasing volume of names within the streets sections of Kelly's directories caused problems. These problems were partially solved by the omission of some inhabitants, but on what basis this selection was made Kelly never specified. The methods of obtaining information varied from publisher to publisher and through time. Usually they involved either visiting houses, or sending or leaving circulars to be filled in by the householders, a system that persisted well into the twentieth century.

Collections of directories are to be found in a great many places, both at a local level and at a national one. As with many other similar sources, such as newspapers and electoral registers, your local studies library or local archive will have a collection for its immediate area. County record offices similarly will have a col-

'Obscenity can be found in every book except the telephone directory.'
GEORGE BERNARD SHAW
(1856–1950)

Defining idea…

lection for the county. Guildhall Library in London has an exceptional collection for the whole country, as does the British Library in Euston. The Historical Directories project (www.historicaldirectories.org) has an ongoing project to publish online directories for England and Wales only between 1750 and 1919.

Historic copies of the *Yellow Pages*, the modern equivalent of directories, at least as far as trades and professions are concerned, are held at the Berkshire Record Office in Reading. On a slightly different tack, BT Archives in London has a near complete set of telephone directories for the whole country produced not only by British Telecom but also by its predecessors, including Post Office Telecommunications, the National Telephone Company and other private companies. These date back to 1880, the year after the public telephone service was introduced into Great Britain.

Q   **Looking though a 1910 directory, I was disappointed to find that** *How did*
     number 27 was missing from the road where my family used to *it go?*
     live. I know from a birth certificate that it was the family home
     in 1908 and the numbers either side – 25 and 29 – were still there
     in the directory so 27 must still have been there because all the
     houses would have been built at the same time. Why would this
     be?

A   *As more directories were produced, people often became annoyed at being*
     continually pestered for information, with the consequence that they did
     not respond to the agents' enquiries. Try looking for other directories,
     either a few years either side of 1910 or perhaps published by another
     company, as these may include the information you are looking for.

Q   **An eccentric great-uncle of mine swears he unwittingly moved**
     into a house that was once the scene of a bloody crime of pas-
     sion, but he refuses to say more. Even my parents don't know if
     he's serious. How can I call his bluff?

A   *If you know the address and you can find the relevant local directories*
     going back year on year, you'll be able to track the owners or occupiers
     of the house. Cross-referencing those names and dates with stories in the
     local papers should give you the answers you're after.

15

Votes and voters

Although not all of us were able to vote until 1929, if you know who could vote, where, and when, then another potential source of information about your ancestors becomes available.

As with many historical records, getting the best from electoral records requires a little knowledge about their background: why and when they were generated and, specifically, what the qualifications were to vote, as these changed with changing legislation.

The 1696 Act for regulating elections was the main drive for the publication of Poll Books. This provided that sheriffs were responsible for compiling a record of the poll in county elections and that those returning officers should make these records available to all. These Poll Books are the books in which the votes cast at parliamentary elections were recorded. Not only were polls *not* secret, but people's names were published together with how they voted. To those of us brought up in the twentieth century, in the age of the secret ballot, the gathering of records about

Here's an idea for you... **Locating where someone was living during the twentieth century can be difficult. Try buying any relevant birth, death or marriage certificate. This will give you an address to check against the electoral registers for your ancestors.**

individuals' political preferences may seem strange but the publication of Poll Books continued right up to the Ballot Act of 1872.

The Poll Books contain the name and address and sometimes occupation of the voter, or the address of the 'freehold' (property) that entitled the voter to his vote. Occasionally there are also snippets of 'extra' information, such as the listing of religious dissenters, Roman Catholics or paupers.

Voters Lists and Freeholders Registers give similar information to the Poll Books but do not record how people voted. Some records also remain of the additions and removals from the lists of those entitled to vote, together with qualifications for being able to vote.

The Sheriff's Lists were books compiled annually and they contain the names and residences of every male freeholder in his county. This was kept for the purposes of summoning juries. Where they survive, they also complement the Poll Books for lists of freeholders.

Before the 1872 Ballot Act introduced the secret ballot, voters were required to physically stand up and declare publicly their electoral allegiance. The fear of going against their landlords' wishes resulted in a substantial number of candidates returned being the landlords, their relatives or cronies. There were many cases of tenants being evicted because they dared to oppose the local landowner. The Poll Books were printed by private entrepreneurs, who were assured of a profit from such a venture because interest in the Books extended beyond just those involved in local politics.

The 1832 Reform Act greatly widened the franchise, and enacted that the names of all those qualified to vote be published annually. The resulting Electoral Registers continue to this day. However, many people were disappointed because voting in the boroughs was restricted to men who occupied homes with an annual rateable value of £10. This resulted in only one in seven adult males qualifying to vote. Nor were the constituencies of equal size. Whereas 35 constituencies had less than 300 electors, Liverpool had a constituency of over 11,000.

In 1910, the government decided to survey every property in England and Wales. Owners, occupiers, values and descriptions of the properties are all recorded, with even the occasional rough plan. To find out how your ancestors were living in 1910, explore IDEA 42, *The Lloyd George Domesday*.

Try another idea…

In 1867, the vote was given, in boroughs, to all householders who had been in residence for at least one year and to all lodgers paying £10-a-year rent; in counties, to all occupiers of houses rated at £12. In 1884, the county franchise was brought into line with the boroughs. Even then only 59% of the adult male population could vote. Women could only vote if they had the relevant property qualifications. In 1918 the property qualification was abolished and all men, and women aged 30 and over, were enfranchised. There wasn't universal suffrage until 1929, when everyone over 21 could vote. Minimum details given in Voters Registers include full names of electors, and place of residence. Pre-1919 registers may also include the 'qualification' for voting.

For local and family historians, Poll Books can offer an insight into the way their ancestors voted, with the possible bonus of occupations and addresses. For the more serious researcher it is possible to study the voting allegiances across a wide geographical area, occupational groups, social strata or timescales.

'Vote early and vote often.'
AL CAPONE (1899–1947)

Defining idea…

How did it go?

Q **Where will I find Poll Books and Electoral Registers?**

A *Separate electoral registers are produced for each constituency and compiled annually. They are organised by address so to get optimum use of them you really do need to know where someone was living. A local copy of the Voters Lists will be found at the local library or archives: a national set is kept at the British Library and is also available commercially on the internet. County record offices, archives and local libraries hold collections of Poll Books relating to their own areas. The British Library, Guildhall Library and the Institute of Historical Research also have large collections of Poll Books. Some of the rarer Poll Books are also commercially available on CD. Freeholders Registers and Sheriff's Lists can be located at the relevant County Record Office or Archives.*

Q **Besides women [until 1929] who else was excluded from voting in parliamentary elections?**

A *There is quite a long list: basically, anyone under 21 (prior to 1969, 18 thereafter); plus, at various times, peers of the realm and peeresses (except 1918–1963); lunatics; sentenced criminals in prison; aliens who were not naturalised; those in receipt of public alms (paupers); anyone convicted of bribery at an election; and those not included in an electoral register (after they were introduced 1832). Certain occupations were also excluded, including serving policemen (before 1887), postmasters and Customs & Excise men (until 1918) and conscientious objectors (1918–1923).*

16

Taxing the community

Taxation is as old as time, and that's just as well from the historians' perspective because tax records offer a wealth of information about the lives of our ancestors.

The Greeks and Romans complained about taxation. Jesus was born in a stable in Bethlehem, as Mary and Joseph were registering for taxation. Lady Godiva rode naked through the streets of Coventry to induce her husband to abolish local taxation.

Over the years, government and the church applied taxes to just about anything and everything, in an attempt to raise revenue to fund their activities. As they did so, complex systems of record keeping evolved.

Many of the early tax records give extensive lists of names, providing us with early 'census' substitutes. Not only can they give you information about an individual but also about relationships. They also give actual addresses and details about property. This can include the individuals' houses, servants, horses, carts and dogs, painting a glorious picture of the way they lived and fitted into their community.

The Domesday Book must be one of the earliest surviving records of land and property but taxation on these really began in earnest in 1692. Money was required 'for carrying on a vigorous war against France'. Church Rates were another such tax levied until 1868.

Poll taxes were essentially taxes levied on individuals. The most notable were those collected between 1377 and 1380, and were a contributory cause of the 1381 Peasants' Revolt. Many Tudor and Stuart subsidies included a poll tax on foreigners or religious dissenters – they paid double.

With a need to raise revenue after the restoration of Charles II as King, Hearth Money was first levied in 1662. The tax was calculated by the number of hearths there were in a building. For the first time, tax inspectors could visit a property. Attempts to avoid paying by blocking up a chimney, if discovered, resulted in paying double.

Hearth Tax was replaced in 1696 by Window Tax, to offset the growing inflation caused by the various conflicts in Ireland and Europe. This was less intrusive than the Hearth Tax as the windows could be counted from the outside. Nonetheless, it was unpopular; its opponents thought it a tax on light and fresh air. People managed to dodge payment by bricking in windows, camouflaging them or even building dummy windows to confuse the inspectors. The tax continued until 1851, when it was replaced by a tax akin to the present day 'council tax' or local property tax.

Around the same time, Parliament brought in legislation requiring the registration of births,

Here's an idea for you...

Many archives now have a searchable catalogue – sometimes even available online. Check out just what taxation records have survived for your areas of interest. You may even find a pro forma 'tax certificate' for one of your ancestors from the eighteenth century.

marriages and burials, which took effect from 1695 to 1700. The idea was to raise new revenue to fund the war of the Spanish succession. Bachelors and widowers were to pay but not spinsters and widows; payment was graduated according to status. The Act required births to be registered within five days and recorded on certificates for each parish but there was nothing specified as to what should happen to the certificates.

Those you think should have left wills often didn't, and those that you think wouldn't often did. To investigate what your ancestor was really worth, start by looking at IDEA 23, *Where there's a will.*

Try another idea…

The government during the second half of the eighteenth century was tireless in its efforts to generate income from the gentry and middle classes. Just as we have to pay taxes or obtain licences or certificates for various activities, so did our ancestors. Hair Powder Duty was levied under a 1794/5 Act – a tax on hair powder payable by those who used it. The list of taxable items is never ending. So we have 'carriage tax', a tax on clocks and watches, dogs, households employing servants, Game Duty on those killing or selling game (including gamekeepers), guns, horses, and silver plate. There were also several general taxes, the most important being County Rates, raised from 1793 to take the place of previous miscellaneous payments and Poor Rate levied by the parish overseers of the poor.

Income tax was introduced in 1799, as a means of paying for the Napoleonic wars. The cost of war had drained Britain's resources, and run up a considerable national debt. The army was starving, and poor conditions in the navy had led to a mutiny. It was repealed several times only to appear as a permanent feature in 1842.

'The avoidance of taxes is the only intellectual pursuit that still carries any reward.'
JOHN MAYNARD KEYNES
(1883-1946)

Defining idea…

Some of the rates and taxes mentioned here we still pay – incorporated within income tax, local rates and VAT. There were exemptions on some of these taxes, which of course generated more lists of names in their own right.

How did it go?

Q Were women ever taxed?

A *Even prior to the Married Women's Property Act (1882) there were many examples when a woman could be taxed – although these usually only applied to widows and spinsters as they were eligible to own property in their own right.*

Q So how do I access some of these taxation records?

A *A lot of these local taxation records can be found amongst the Quarter Sessions records, deposited at local archives. The Quarter Sessions were the quarterly meetings of Justices of the Peace who met to deal with many local administrative issues and hear local criminal cases. Justices made decisions on anything and everything from murder to the failure of a tradesman to display his name on the side of a cart. They would preside over cases ranging from disorderly singing, bankruptcy and witchcraft to a wide range of administrative tasks, including the maintenance of highways, the granting of licences and permits, relief of the poor, bastardy orders, registration of boats and barges and, of course, the collecting of local taxes. Many of these records have been transcribed and indexed by local and family history societies or record societies and may be available to purchase.*

17

How does the land lie?

The maps and plans of Britain are a cornucopia of landscape information. Plot the geographical changes in your community and see how it grows.

Our environment is constantly changing as ancient historic sites disappear: woodland, farms, whole villages come and go. Even in towns, Victorian terraces are replaced by modern estates and superstores.

The significance of maps and plans does not stop with raw landscape information because those changes in the landscape came about because of historical and social change. Hence, their value in providing a series of contemporaneous snapshots detailing features created before the date of the survey cannot be overemphasised. Much of the detailed information will depend on the scale used but all maps and plans are valuable sources for researching the evolution of a street, farm, estate, village or town.

Evidence of Celtic field systems, the Roman roads and villas, the village sites of the Dark Ages, Norman castles and Tudor enclosures can often be identified, even on modern maps. Later events, such as famous battles, are obviously more clearly

Here's an idea for you...

To see how really useful and informative maps and plans can be, and how relatively easy they are to use, pick somewhere you are interested in and just see what maps and plans your local record office has for that place and what period they cover. Scan the internet, too, where you will find several websites that include digitised old maps, particularly early Ordnance Survey maps, as well as current maps and even aerial photographs.

documented so names like Sebastopol Terrace and Trafalgar Farm can point to development at a fairly precise date. The pattern of streets in areas urbanised or developed during recent decades usually still preserve the pattern of fields created in earlier centuries, possibly by the Enclosure Awards or at a much earlier time.

A symbol of the landowners' status, maps were hand-drawn by hired surveyors before the Ordnance Survey came into place in 1791. During the eighteenth century there was a revolution in county map-making, with most new maps being based on a system of scientific triangulation. The Trigonometrical Survey of the Board of Ordnance, later to become the Ordnance Survey, was founded on 21 June 1791, with the objective of mapping the southeast of England. By 1840 the survey had covered much of the rest of Great Britain, south of the Hull–Preston line, mostly at a scale of two inches to the mile (1:31,680).

During the period 1805 to 1874, what became known as the 'Old Series' was published in a total of 110 sheets at a scale of one inch to the mile (1:63,360). The second, or 'New Series', also produced at one inch to the mile, was published in a total of 360 sheets from the 1870s to 1899. Further editions followed, including the popular 'One-inch Popular Edition' following the end of the First

Defining idea...

'God made the country, and man made the town.'
WILLIAM COWPER (1731–1800)
The Task

World War. Between 1974 and 1976, maps at a scale of 2 cm to 1 km (1:50,000) were introduced, and named the *Landranger Series* from 1979.

These smaller scale maps are very useful, but it is the much larger scales (also produced by the Ordnance Survey) that really come into their own for studying the past of a particular locality. From 1840, towns with a population of over 4,000 in northern England and Scotland were also surveyed at a scale of five feet to the mile (1:1056); and between 1844 and 1853, London and some other towns were also covered at this scale, and even at ten feet to the mile (1:528). These can show incredible detail, down to pillar boxes, cab stands and lampposts. In 1854, a scale of 1:2500 (just over twenty-five inches to the mile) was introduced for cultivated areas, and in May 1855, a 1:500 scale (1056 feet to the mile) was prescribed for all urban areas.

In many ways, old maps are every bit as attractive as other *objets d'art* and it can be tempting to see them as nothing other than that. But in Britain we have been blessed with a long tradition of highly accurate map and plan making at a variety of scales, particularly from the first Ordnance Survey in 1791. They can bring the past landscapes back into view and be a vital resource for both household and local history. Maps and plans will not show you a continuous unravelling of the changes through time, but they will provide a series of very detailed descriptions of places, from streets to parishes and beyond, at many particular points in history, both distant and recent.

The National Farm Survey and the Records of the Valuation Office both have series of definitive maps associated with them. Find out more in IDEA 42, *The Lloyd George Domesday* and IDEA 43, *The National Farm Survey*.

Try another idea…

'*Maps encourage boldness. They're like cryptic love letters. They make anything seem possible.*'
MARK JENKINS, travel columnist and writer, *To Timbuktu*

Defining idea…

How did it go?

Q **I managed to get hold of some wonderful old Ordnance Survey maps at a car boot sale that show the area where I live before the developers moved in. I'd really like to know what was there before the 1930s, which is the date of the oldest maps I've got. The local studies department at my library does have some early Ordnance Survey maps but nothing earlier than mine. What can I do?**

A *Make a trip to your local County Record Office, where they will have all sorts of plans, such as the mid-nineteenth century tithe maps and probably much earlier estate plans, sales particulars for the big estates and perhaps plans attached to deeds and mortgages from very early times. Most record offices have their catalogue available online so you can make some investigations before you go.*

Q **I've got quite a few maps of my area going back a long way but it's very difficult to follow all the development because they're in so many different forms and scales. Any suggestions as to how I could clarify my collection?**

A *Try to download digitised copies of what you've already got, and any other missing pieces of the puzzle. If you have the skills and the equipment, scan the hard copies into your computer. Then, adjust the scales of the maps on screen so they're all the same. You can then produce a series of overlays so you can see very clearly how change and development took place. It's really not as difficult as it may sound ... honest!*

18

Become a where wolf

Begin your prowl and discover what's found where within the giant labyrinth of archives, libraries and record repositories.

The records of the British peoples are said to 'excel all others in age, beauty, correctness and authority', with records that run in virtually unbroken series from the eleventh century to the present day.

For anyone interested in their own past or in their country's heritage, there are immensely rich veins of information to be unearthed. The National Archives (TNA) of England, Wales and the United Kingdom has one of the largest archival collections in the world, spanning 1000 years of British history, from the Domesday Book of 1086 to government papers recently released to the public. These are the records created by central government and they range from some of Britain's most famous and dramatic events, such as the Jack the Ripper murders and the sinking of the Titanic, to personal and private histories. Immigration and emigration records are

Here's an idea for you...

Make a visit to your local record offices. They can cover the whole spectrum of family and local history, and their experienced staff will guide you to deeds, maps, photographs, possibly copies of the Victorian census returns and much else. You'll be amazed what you can discover. Make sure you check the opening times before you go though.

also available, as are records of the two World Wars and records of crime and punishment.

The National Archives was formed in 2003, when the Public Record Office (PRO) and the Historical Manuscripts Commission amalgamated. The PRO itself was established by Act of Parliament in 1838, with the primary purpose of preserving the records of the law courts, but it very quickly became used by other government departments for the deposit of administrative records. The Scottish Record Office and The Public Record Office of Northern Ireland are independent bodies and hold their own records.

Among the records held at TNA are:

- Armed service personnel and operational records; medals and gallantry awards
- A number of occupational records
- Post-1834 Poor Law records
- Lists of taxpayers
- Ships' passenger lists
- Naturalisations and denizations
- Changes of name
- Records of emigrants and immigrants
- Divorce records
- Records about companies and businesses
- Registered designs and trade marks; patents of invention
- Records of the central civil and criminal courts
- Maps
- Assize court records; records of prisoners; transportation records
- Records of land transfer
- Records of Crown manors

If your research suggests your family underwent a major upheaval at some point, the local paper at that time might shed more light on the reasons. Check out IDEA 9, *All the news that's fit to print.*

Try another idea…

Important as TNA is, many, if not most, of the records you will require are held at a local level. Every county has it own record office (sometimes more than one) and nearly every borough and town has its own local studies library. It is in these that you will find records created by local authorities, business papers, workhouse records, electoral registers

'History: an account mostly false, of events unimportant, which are brought about by rulers mostly naves, and soldiers mostly fools.'
AMBROSE BIERCE (1842–?1914)
American short story writer and journalist

Defining idea…

and poll books, manorial court rolls, school records, photographs, maps and even collections of private papers and letters.

Most county record offices double up as the diocesan record office and so will hold the important collections of parish registers of baptisms, marriages and burials and other parish chest material, pre-1858 wills and other records for which the parish, archdeaconry or diocese were responsible.

Other important collections of records include those held at the Parliamentary Archives (the records of Parliament are not public records); those at the British Library; at the Imperial War Museum, National Army Museum and National Maritime Museum; and in University Libraries. Records of professional organisations and societies often have their own archive, as do some of the major nonconformist groups. Many of the great land-owning families have their own muniments rooms, which can contain details of sub-tenants, leaseholders and staff, as well as of the family itself. Over a thousand charters survive from the early kings and are held at the British Library.

The diversity of our documentary heritage means that anyone who wants to delve into their past, to research their ancestry or the history of their home, village or town is guaranteed an abundance of riches.

Q   **I'm a bit overwhelmed by the number of possible archives, libraries and record offices that may have what I want – or may not. Is there a way of finding which are going to be the most likely to be able help me with my search for my roots? I haven't got the time to visit them all on the off-chance.**

How did it go?

A   *Yet again the World Wide Web comes to our rescue. Nearly every major archive – national, local or private – has its own website detailing its holdings. The National Archives website contains a wealth of information, not only on its own collections. Through this website, there is access to many hundreds of other record offices and archives, to listings of their holdings, and to their contact details. A veritable Pandora's box of goodies.*

Q   **I've been told that I cannot see some records because they are 'closed'. What does that mean?**

A   *The Freedom of Information Act came into effect from 1 January 2005 giving the right of access to information held by many public bodies. Some records, though, for very good reasons, do remain with a statutory closure period in force. The record office should be able to give you specific information and there is guidance on The National Archives website.*

19

Files, formats and family trees

Clarity, Convenience and Completeness are the golden rules for organising your research. Living by them might be difficult, but the benefits are well worth the effort.

If cleanliness is next to godliness, then neatness cannot be far behind.

I have a cupboard. It houses the results of my many years of research into my past. It is organised in a series of smart lever-arch files, uniformly labelled and colour-coded. The pages within are all neatly typed with the pages cross-referenced. Everything is easy to find and I am proud of my collection. I am dreaming.

It is so very easy to fall foul of the desire to research and research with little realisation of the need to record your findings systematically, thoroughly and carefully, and to then file them in such a way that they can be easily recovered and used by you and those who will come after you. So what do you need to consider?

Here's an idea for you... **You can buy all manner of blank forms into which to enter the results of your research. But why not design your own? Apart from being considerably cheaper, they can be customised to suit your filing system and your personal needs.**

ONE – BEFORE YOU BEGIN

Where am I? Which library? What record office? What is the date? What am I looking for? Great-aunt Matilda who? Have I got a headache or left my reading glasses at home?

TWO – THE RECORD

What am I looking at? Is it a book, microfilm, an original, a website? Does it have a title? What is its reference number? Is it a transcript, abstract, extract or something else that may be incomplete? Are there missing pages, torn pages, gaps in the record? How easy is it for me to read? Easy-peasy: it's in Latin, and it was written by an arthritic monk!

THREE – THE SEARCH

What/who am I looking for? Am I searching the whole thing or just part of it – specific time period, particular chapter, only the index? Am I looking for all occurrences of a surname or place or only for a very specific event? What variants, if any, of the name am I looking for?

FOUR – TAKING DOWN THE INFORMATION

What did I not find? This is just as important to note as what you did find, because you do not want to waste time in the future not finding it for a second time.

One of the best ways to copy information is to take a photograph of it, so see IDEA 49, *Cameras are not just for holidays!*

Try another idea…

Transcribe everything exactly: do not abbreviate and do not expand – 'Mgt.' Brown stays as 'Mgt.' so don't write down 'Margaret' because it might have been 'Mry.'. 'Buckinghamshire' stays as just that and not 'Bucks' or in six years' time you will read it as 'Berks'. Note down any omissions or gaps. If you can't read something or are unsure of a word or two, then write yourself a note to say so; or speak nicely to a member of staff who may be able to help you.

There is a certain law that says you will find what you want just as the librarian announces 'We are closing in five minutes'. There is every temptation to rush to get something finished. In fact there is always the temptation to get everything down as quickly as possible so you can get on to the next item. Not a good idea, as from such keenness do mistakes arise. Take deep breaths and slow down: the books, films, records will be there tomorrow – they have nowhere else to go.

'Exactness and neatness in moderation is a virtue, but carried to extremes narrows the mind.'
FRANCOIS DE SALIGNAC FENELON (1651–1715) French theologian, author

Defining idea…

Nearly all libraries, record offices and the like allow you to use laptops and PDAs – although you should ask first – but if you are a two-finger typist then errors when inputting will undoubtedly happen. It is therefore doubly important that you check very carefully what you have entered before you go home.

FIVE – AT HOME

Try to analyse your findings as soon as you can, while your recent discoveries are still clear in your mind, because then you will realise any failings in your note-taking. Come up with a system of filing and storing that suits *you*. There is no right way, although there are several things you do need to consider. Consistency is the key word here: this covers areas such as size of paper, referencing systems, organisation of the papers (by name, by family, by place, by date – whatever suits you). If you are using a computer program to record your information, much the same applies.

Always remember to 'back-up'. And not only if you are keeping everything on computer – a second copy of the results of your toils should always be kept in a separate location, just in case …

Defining idea… **'Good order is the foundation of all things.'**
EDMUND BURKE (1729–1797)

Q   **I have found this really interesting deed that I know mentions one of my forebears – at least I think it is interesting but I can't really read it because of the awful old handwriting. The archivist insists that it is not written in Hebrew. What can I do?**

How did it go?

A   *See if you can get a photocopy of the deed and then apply a modicum of perseverance. You will certainly be able to make out a word or two and bear in mind that there are only 26 letters in the alphabet. You'll be surprised how soon you can build up further words and then whole sentences.*

Q   **That went not at all well. Any other ideas?**

A   *The National Archives website has a whole section dedicated to palaeography (reading old handwriting) and another to Latin. Here you can learn all the tricks in a really fun way and within no time at all you will become much more competent. Or join a family or local history society where other members will certainly be able to help you.*

20

Fancy a date?

All dates are not the same so it is important that you understand the old dating practices in order to date documents correctly.

Given that it was only in 1752 that England adopted the 'modern' Gregorian calendar, it is vital to get the background on dates and learn how to determine when an event actually happened.

Until 1752, England used the Julian calendar that had been introduced in Rome in 46 BC. Each year officially ran from Lady Day (25 March) to 24 March. By 1751, the Julian calendar, which was based on a nominal 'year' of 365 days plus an extra day every four years, was 11 days out of step with the Gregorian calendar. This error had first been recognised early in the sixteenth century, but it wasn't until 1582 that Pope Gregory XIII undertook to correct it. He decreed in a Papal Bull that the day following 4 October 1582 would be 15 October (hence, Gregorian calendar). To avoid the problem recurring, the rule for leap years was also changed such that centenary years that were not divisible by 400 were not leap years.

Here's an idea for you... **To discover which day of the week an event actually took place on, consult a perpetual calendar. The calendar will show, for example, that 25 October 1760 was a Saturday.**

States obedient to the Pope adopted the Gregorian calendar immediately. These were Spain, Portugal, Italy and France. Prussia, the Catholic States of Germany, Holland and Flanders adopted it in 1583; Catholic parts of Switzerland in 1583/84; Poland in 1586; Hungary in 1587; the German and Netherlands Protestant states and Denmark in 1700; and Sweden in 1753.

An Act of Parliament, Lord Chesterfield's Act of 1751, finally replaced the Julian calendar with the Gregorian calendar in England and Wales, bringing them in line with the rest of Europe. The Act stated that 1 January should be the first day of the year. Thus 1750 had commenced on 25 March 1750 and ended 24 March 1750/51, while 1751 commenced 25 March 1751 and ended on 31 December 1751. The changes were to apply to all the Dominions of the British Crown. Christmas Day remained as 25 December, even though the true anniversary was now 6 January. Banks chose to ignore this shorter year and continued with 365 days, so that the financial year now ended on 5 April (11 days after 25 March), which has continued to the present day.

For the 170 years between the Papal Bull of Gregory XIII and 1752, the two calendars had been used side by side in Western Europe. Thus communication in Europe was prone to ambiguities as far as dates were concerned. Even within England, a year starting on 1 January (known as the historical year) was in general use for almanacs etc., and 1 January had always been celebrated as New Year's Day. The year starting

25 March was called the Civil or Legal Year, although the phrase Old Style was commonly used. These ambiguities are not just a problem for modern researchers; they were a contemporary problem for which contemporary solutions were required. Prior to 1752, dates between 1 January and 24 March each year were expressed, for example, as 1 February 1700/01, written to show that the date was 1 February 1700 in the old style but February 1701 in the new style – an attempt to try and differentiate between the old and new calendar.

Ambiguities continued in Eastern Europe into the twentieth century. Russia and Turkey converted to the Gregorian calendar in 1918, Yugoslavia and Romania in 1919 and Greece in 1923. Thus the October Revolution 'happened' in what was November and Christmas is celebrated in Russia in January, the old calendar being used when determining the dates of religious festivals. Japan adopted the Gregorian calendar in 1872. China started to use the Gregorian calendar for official and business purposes in 1912, but the traditional Chinese lunar calendar continues to be used for most personal matters, such as the celebration of birthdays and festivals, including when to celebrate the Chinese New Year.

Using maps from a number of different dates, you can plot the geographical changes in your community and see how it grew and changed over time. See IDEA 17, *How does the land lie?*

Try another idea…

'Don't be fooled by the calendar. There are only as many days in the year as you make use of. One man gets only a week's value out of a year while another man gets a full year's value out of a week.'

Defining idea…

CHARLES DOW RICHARDS
(1879–1956)
New Brunswick politician

How did it go?

Q   What are Regnal years?

A   *Early parish registers, manorial and legal records were dated using regnal years. This type of dating system started with the date of accession of each sovereign. For example, George III became King on 25 October 1760, thus '3 George III' would refer to the third year of King George's reign and run from 25 October 1762 to 24 October 1763. There are exceptions to the rule, the main ones being King Charles II, whose reign was deemed to have commenced on his father's execution in 1649 and not when he actually sat on the throne after the restoration of the monarchy in 1660, and King George II, because of the changes to the calendar during his reign in 1752. The use of regnal years decreased over time and they are now rarely used.*

Q   I have seen reference to special or feast days. What are these?

A   *Older documents often record events by reference to feast or Saint days, such as St Swithin's Day (15 July) or St Lucy's Day (13 December), the shortest day before the new calendar was introduced. You also had the Quarter days when rents were due. These were Lady Day (25 March), Mid-Summers or St John's Day (24 June), Michaelmas (29 September) and Christmas Day (25 December). Lammas Day, on 1 August, was when fences were removed from common land to allow grazing by livestock until the land was re-seeded again. Many of these days were pagan in origin.*

21

On the move

**Follow the branches of your family's migrations – they
may stretch further and wider than you think.**

*One of the times of greatest population
movement was during the Industrial
Revolution.*

Although historians may disagree over exactly when the Industrial Revolution
began and ended, most consider it to have lasted from the mid-eighteenth century
until the end of the nineteenth century. Whatever the view, the many new and
interesting inventions and improvements to the transport infrastructure trans-
formed the British Isles from a mainly rural to a more urban population. These
times saw the development of factories and mills, canals and railways, and the
demise of many of the rural cottage industries.

It is not surprising, therefore, to discover just how mobile our ancestors were.
Although some families stayed within a relatively small area, many did not, gradually moving through the country motivated by economic necessity, employment or
trade. Merchants and others involved in trading could move around the country to
maintain their livelihoods.

The commencement of civil registration in 1837 partnered by the ten-yearly census returns allows you to track your ancestors' movements during the latter half of the nineteenth century relatively easily with the use of the internet.

However, what do you do before that date? An ancestor may appear in a parish in one of the large cities like Liverpool or London but how do you discover from whence he came? The first entry relating to a person in a parish register may indicate his origins. Marriage entries after 1754 should record the place of residence of each spouse. Banns registers, allegations or bonds for marriage licences should also note the place of residence of both parties. It is important to gather information on any extended family that you can find within that parish to help you with your quest.

The International Genealogical Index (IGI) produced by the Church of Jesus Christ of Latter-day Saints is an online database containing over 700 million entries, mainly baptisms and marriages, taken from worldwide sources. It can open up many new possibilities for you. Although it is not fully comprehensive, the IGI can be a fantastic 'finding' aid. Most counties have a baptism or marriage index that may reveal the origins of an ancestor. Often, these have been compiled by family history societies. There is also a National Burial Index, an ongoing project to complement the IGI, so if you cannot locate the burial of an ancestor you may find them in a previously unknown family grave.

Here's an idea for you...

If you are struggling to locate an ancestor in a particular area before civil registration was introduced, double check that you haven't overlooked any major indexes covering that part of the country. You might find him or her there.

A person's will might disclose his or her place of origin, or it may refer to previous places of residence. The will may list legacies of land and property far away from where the testator died, some of which may give a hint as to an origin. Title deeds to property can give evidence of an ancestor owning land in several parishes, which may open up other avenues.

Apprenticeship records often indicate an apprentice's place of origin. Parish sources that may record an ancestor's movement between different parishes include removal orders and settlement certificates. Overseer's records of payment to the poor or payment of tithes can indicate when someone arrived in an area. Directories are useful for tracking the movements of tradespeople, while the records of freemen, guilds or livery companies may reveal places not only where someone traded but also from whence they came.

Other records worth consulting that may also give a place of birth include professional and employment records, military records, court records, school or university records, monumental inscriptions and newspaper obituaries or reports of crime.

These are just some of the sources that may help you with your research. However, once you find a potential candidate from one of these, you really do need to look for collaborating evidence. When using any index, be sure to seek out the original record from which the information was gathered – most of which will be found at the local county record office – for confirmation, accuracy and to make sure that nothing has been missed.

There is usually some veracity in any family story, but establishing which parts are true and which aren't can be a problem. For more on this see IDEA 3, *Show and tell*.

Try another idea…

'Curiosity is one of the most permanent and certain characteristics of a vigorous intellect.'
SAMUEL JOHNSON (1709–1784)
lexicographer, critic and poet

Defining idea…

How did
it go?

Q **I have located the baptism of an ancestor in a large city. However, all his siblings were baptised elsewhere. Can you explain
why?**

A *You need to step back and take a broad look at the extended family to
see whether there was any family connection with the city. Did they own
property there? What was the father's occupation – could that have caused
the family to move temporarily? Or were they just passing through? Often
women returned 'home' to mother to give birth – especially for a first child
– so that may be worth looking at as well.*

Q **My ancestor has a fairly unusual surname and I can't find anyone
else in the area with that surname. Why might that be?**

A *Have you checked to see if anyone is doing a one-name study of your
surname – that is, collecting all references world wide? If someone is doing
such a study, they may have information about your ancestor and his origins. It is also worth checking if anyone else is researching the same family
in the same or adjoining counties. They too may have useful information.
Many family history societies also run 'strays' indexes. A stray is a recorded
event in which a person is described in the source record as being from, or
connected with, a place outside the area in which they normally lived or
were born.*

22

Open the doors and see the people

For centuries, the Church has kept registers of baptisms, marriages and burials. They can very effectively open up a window on the lives of our forebears.

Extracts from parish registers:

Odiham, Hampshire — marriages, 14 January 1745: Charles Hambleton (afterwards proved to be a woman) married Mary Scarnel

Lanchester — baptisms, 1 October 1815: Thomas Wardrobe, illegitimate son of Isabella Try-em-all, single woman

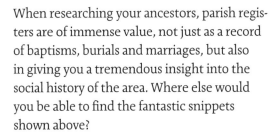

Bishop's Transcripts were copies of the parish registers, usually sent annually from 1597 to the Bishop. However, there are many cases where there are considerable differences between the two, so always check any entries extracted from the original registers with the transcripts and vice versa.

When researching your ancestors, parish registers are of immense value, not just as a record of baptisms, burials and marriages, but also in giving you a tremendous insight into the social history of the area. Where else would you be able to find the fantastic snippets shown above?

Parish registers were first ordered to be kept in Spain in 1497. It wasn't until 1538, however, that parish registers reached the British Isles. Thomas Cromwell, Henry VIII's Vicar-General, decided that formal records should be kept in England and Wales, his main reasons being to provide evidence for inheritance purposes, to prevent forbidden marriages (e.g. incestuous) and to calculate the population for tax purposes.

It was decreed that the registers were to be completed by every Church on a weekly basis. However, the standards of record keeping varied tremendously, depending on who was actually responsible for doing it, leading to considerable variation in the quality of the registers of different churches. From 1597 events were to be recorded in parchment books.

Record keeping only really started to improve with Hardwicke's Marriage Act from 1754, which required separate printed books for marriages and the publishing of banns or the production of a marriage licence. Banns, or intentions of marriage, were published for three consecutive Sundays prior to marriage and recorded in a separate banns register. If you are struggling to locate a marriage, check the banns register, as it will give the details of where the marriage actually took place. A marriage licence (actually the allegation or bond – the licence itself rarely survives) can also give you additional information. The allegation will give the full names of parties, residence and marital status. It may also give the couple's ages and the name of the church in which the marriage could take place. Additionally, the bond sometimes gives the groom's profession. Reasons for marrying by licence varied. One was speed – useful for people going abroad or those 'with child'. William Shakespeare and Anne Hathaway applied for a licence seven months prior to their first child's christening. Another was confidentiality: you could marry (or re-marry) more discreetly, without the need to publish banns.

There is more to life than just being born, married or dying. To really bring someone to life, look at IDEA 16, *Taxing the community*, to discover what else your ancestors got up to.

Try another idea...

Generally, the earlier the register, the less information will be recorded. In the earliest registers, a baptism may record only the father's name. Even into the eighteenth century, it is not uncommon to see baptismal

'Life is so constructed that an event does not, cannot, will not, match the expectation.'
CHARLOTTE BRONTE (1816–1855)

Defining idea...

entries as limited as 'John son of William Easingwood'. The recording of mothers' names wasn't commonplace until the late seventeenth century. Where mothers' names are recorded, their maiden name is rarely given, the exception being nonconformist registers and 'Dade' registers. Dade registers of baptisms and burials (mainly for the Diocese of York from 1777–1812) include information on several generations of a family. Details of residence and father's occupation will appear from the early 1700s.

Rose's Act of 1812 extended the use of pre-printed registers to baptisms and burials. For baptisms, these required the name of the child, forenames and (married) surname of the parents, residence and occupation of the father. In addition to the required date of baptism, some ministers helpfully recorded the date of birth or age. Illegitimacy will be clearly indicated by any one of a variety of terms. The name of the reputed father will sometimes be included. Even after 1812, baptismal registers rarely give the mother's maiden name. Burial registers usually only give you the name and age of the deceased, and their residence.

Everything, of course, changed with the introduction of civil registration in 1837.

Q **So, if the recording of parish registers in England and Wales began in 1538, have they all survived?**

How did it go?

A *Only about 700 (of 11,000) parishes have registers going back to 1538. In 1976, it was reported to the House of Lords that since 1831, 2,400 volumes of parish registers had disappeared. Where the original parish registers haven't survived, you can of course look at the Bishop's Transcripts. Also, check if one of the recording societies active during the latter part of the nineteenth century transcribed the registers.*

Q **What do parish registers contain besides the details of baptisms, marriages or burials?**

A *It really depends on who was responsible for maintaining the registers as to what was recorded and thus what you will discover. The front or rear leaves of the book often contain financial information relating to the parish accounts, gifts to the church or other good causes, such as the rebuilding of St Paul's Cathedral after the Great Fire of London. They may also contain names of churchwardens and other parish officers, lists of those taking communion and even detailed lists of parishioners – in reality, a local census taking place perhaps 50 years before the first official national census. It is also common to find information of local interest – for example, descriptions of floods or heavy snow – and many registers contain records of the church spire being struck by lightning and subsequent fire damage to the church.*

23

Where there's a will

Wills have a singular importance, not least because of the detail they frequently contain about family, relationships, property and place of burial.

Those you think should have left wills often didn't; those that you think wouldn't often did. Expect to be both disappointed and pleasantly surprised.

From the 1520s, wills were regularly recorded in the ecclesiastical records and until the mid-nineteenth century, probate (the ratification of a will) was controlled by the Church, as were most matters to do with death, with over 300 Church courts functioning at one time or another. Wills are one of only a handful of documents of a personal nature, apart from diaries, which might give some insight into the innermost feelings of an ancestor:

'… my wife Anne Porter who lives separate and apart from me shall take no benefit nor be entitled nor be interested in any manor under this my will to any part of my estate' (1840)

Here's an idea for you...

The superior ecclesiastical court that was responsible for probate until 1858 was the Prerogative Court of Canterbury (PCC), which covered the whole country. The original records are now held by The National Archives (TNA). All these have been indexed and you can search them online at TNA's website. You can also download digitised copies of the wills for a fee. Many famous wills are included, such as those of Horatio Nelson, William Shakespeare and Jane Austen. So, choose one of your heroes or heroines and for a small fee see what they had to say in their will.

The system of jurisdiction of each probate court is frequently almost incomprehensible. These jurisdictions overlapped with those of other courts and indeed may have changed from time to time. Simply, the court where a will was proved depended on the whereabouts of the deceased's property.

Many, if not most, wills are dated shortly before the death of the testator. There are some possible reasons for this. In those days, you knew if you caught something nasty you were probably on your way out. Possibly, too, the expense put people off from making their only will until the last moment. The thought that writing a will might have been 'tempting fate' is another possible reason. Probate was usually completed within a few weeks of the testator's death, but there are many exceptions to this. Very generally, the whole matter, from the actual making of the will to probate, could take just a matter of weeks.

Probate records include wills, testaments, administrations and inventories. There is a

difference between 'wills' and 'testaments'. Wills relate to real estate; testaments refer to personal goods (clothing, jewellery, household goods, tools of trade, farm animals, stocks and shares, debts, and also cash). The two were generally united in one document, 'My Last Will and Testament', in England and Wales; this was not the case in Scotland or the Channel Islands.

Have look at IDEA 18, *Become a where wolf*, for more information on how to track down a particular document.

Try another idea...

There are no rules as to who might and might not have made a will. Class and fortune (or lack of it) make no difference, and the wills of the well-to-do lie next to those of the ne'er-do-well.

With so many probate courts functioning from the fourteenth century until 1858, it is not surprising that the records themselves are now located in record offices, libraries and other places of deposit across the breadth of the United Kingdom. The difficulty in discovering which court or courts may have had jurisdiction is compounded by the difficulty in determining where any surviving records may now be held.

'The man that leaves no will after his death had little will before his death.'
AUSTIN O'MALLEY (1858–1932)
American oculist
and miscellaneous writer

Defining idea...

'You give but little when you give of your possessions. It is when you give of yourself that you truly give.'
KAHLIL GIBRAN (1883–1931)
Lebanese poet, artist and philosopher

In the main, these records – wills, administrations and inventories – are to be found in the county record offices, which double up as the diocesan record office. There are some exceptions to this, such as the Borthwick Institute in York and the Lichfield Diocesan Record Office in Staffordshire.

From 12 January 1858, all ecclesiastical courts were abolished, and District Probate Registries were set up throughout England and Wales. Since then, the district registries have sent copies of all Grants of Probate, and all wills associated with them, to what is now the Principal Registry of the Family Division in London, where annual centralised indexes have been prepared.

Wills may be one of the few sources that do give us a deep insight into the private lives of our ancestors. For instance, in his will, dated 1790, Charles Smith wrote:

'… Item I give devise and bequeath unto my respectful friend Elizabeth Morgan all my household furniture, stock in trade, ready cash, book debts, notes of hand and all other my estate, and effects of what nature or kind the same may be, to and for her own sole use and benefit Item I give and bequeath unto Frances Smith my wife the sum of one shilling of lawful money of Great Britain …'

Q   **I know it's quite easy to search for a will from 1858 onwards, as they are all one place, at the Principal Registry of the Family Division. But how can I easily discover where earlier wills are kept?**

How did it go?

A   *Fathoming out where to start looking for wills, administrations and other associated documents is a two-stage process. Firstly you have to determine in which court, or courts, the grant may have been made, and then ascertain where the records of that court are now kept. There are several books on 'Probate Jurisdictions' that will help you, and these also give details of where the records are held. But do check with the record office to make certain before visiting.*

Q   **One of my female relatives appears to have gone from riches to rags in circumstances I can only assume mirror those of the wife mentioned in the above extract from Charles Smith's will. How on earth could that happen?**

A   *Such things could occur because the law, until 1882, maintained that a man and his wife were one and, in the absence of a pre-nuptial agreement, all a woman's possessions, even her clothing, belonged to her husband.*

24

Inghamites, Swedenborgians, Muddletonians and others

If we were all the same, it would be a dull world – and when it comes to religion, it's no different. Nonconformist ancestors can add even more depth to your roots.

Whether the degree of religious nonconformity that England and Wales has enjoyed — or suffered, depending on your viewpoint — has been beneficial or a disadvantage to the nation is something academics will continue to debate.

Before 1640, it is unlikely that you will find much, if any, evidence of nonconformity in your family, even if it was there. Before that date, men and women who deliberately separated themselves from the established Church of England were subject to draconian laws introduced by Henry VIII and his daughter Queen Elizabeth. In 1534, England had renounced Papal supremacy and established the Church of England.

Here's an idea for you... **Check out an easy source of all the births/baptisms and marriages – but not deaths/burials – of those nonconformist registers deposited in 1840 and 1857. They are now indexed on the International Genealogical Index (IGI), at least in theory, which can be found on the Latter-day Saints (LDS) website (www.Family Search. com). However, as with all sources, if an entry is found on the IGI, it is vital to check with the original register because much additional information may be given.**

With the Act of Supremacy and Uniformity of 1559, there was complete separation from Rome; fines were imposed on all men who refused to attend Church of England services; and, in 1563, the death penalty was imposed on all priests who said mass. This discrimination against Catholics continued until the Catholic Relief Act of 1778. Consequently, there are few registers surviving for Catholic congregations from before this date and these are still mainly with the church.

Between 1643 and 1660, during the Commonwealth period, the Established Church was Presbyterian and the earliest surviving Protestant nonconformist registers date from this period. Evangelists travelled the country and gained new followers for their own version of Christianity. People moved in and out of nonconformity with considerable ease, changing allegiances as their own beliefs altered, or were altered for them by a particularly effective preacher on the village green. By the late eighteenth century, nonconformists were an accepted part of any parish community. My own ancestor, a Methodist in Wiltshire, served on the parish vestry, and was buried in the parish churchyard.

Defining idea... **'All religions are founded on the fear of the many and the cleverness of the few.'**
STENDHAL, pen-name of Marie Henri Beyle (1783–1842) French novelist, critic and biographer

Following the introduction of civil registration of births, marriages and deaths in 1837, the Registrar General, in 1840 and again in 1857, requested that all nonconformist congregations surrender their registers up to and including 1837. There are relatively few dating from before the eighteenth century; certainly no burials from before 1691. These deposited registers are now part of The National Archives (TNA), with copies at both the Family Records Centre and TNA. Unlike parish registers, these nonconformist registers frequently belonged to the ministers, who took them with them as they travelled around on their 'circuit' or when they transferred to another part of the country. Very often, you can expect to find more information in a nonconformist register than in its Church of England counterpart.

Nonconformists had to be married in the Church of England from 1754–1837, but are frequently buried in the parish churchyard because few nonconformist groups had their own burial grounds. See IDEA 22, *Open the doors and see the people*.

Try another idea...

In a piece like this, it is not possible to discuss all the many nonconformist groups that have existed, or still exist, let alone the extent of their own records and where they are to be found. There are many books available on particular religions and the internet is unlikely to let you down in your search for more specific information. But perhaps particular mention should be made of a few important collections.

The Religious Society of Friends, or Quakers, were exempted under Hardwicke's 1754 Marriage Act because of the excellence of their record keeping and any one with Quaker ancestry is very fortunate. Their main library is at Friends House in London. Dr Williams's Library in London was founded as a register of births for nonconformists in 1742 and some 48,975 births of Protestant dissenters (Baptists, Presbyterians, Unitarians, and Independents or Congregationalists) were registered from 1716 to 1837. The records are now held at The National Archives.

'There is only one religion, though there are a hundred versions of it.'
GEORGE BERNARD SHAW
(1856–1950)

Defining idea...

Bunhill Fields was the site of some 123,000 burials of dissenters between 1665 and 1853. The four-acre burial ground is just north of the City of London. Originally intended for victims of the Great Plague, it was apparently never used for that purpose but became immediately a place used exclusively for nonconformists. With little other option, many nonconformists in London ended up in Bunhill Fields, including three of the most eminent: John Bunyan, William Blake and Daniel Defoe. The records are mainly at Guildhall Library and there are several indexes to parts of the registers.

How did it go?

Q   Are there any obvious indications that some of my ancestors may have been nonconformists?

A   *With the exception of Quakers and Jews, there are no nonconformist marriages from 1755 until 1837. Therefore, if you are finding marriages in the Church of England registers but no baptisms, then this can point to nonconformists. The use of Old Testament names can also be an indicator.*

Q   The registers not deposited in 1840 or 1857 and those for the years following 1837 seem to be difficult to locate. Is there no central listing of their whereabouts?

A   *Even individual sects do not usually keep any form of listing. The best place to start the search is the local county record office. If they do not have them themselves, they may well be able to advise where they might be located.*

25

Daddy, what did *you* do in the war?

Most of our parents and grandparents played a part in the twentieth century wars, even as civilians. Find out what part it was that they played.

The two propaganda images that are most remembered from the First World War are those featuring Kitchener's accusatory finger (Your Country Needs You) and the small girl interrogating her father (Daddy, What Did <u>You</u> Do in the Great War?).

More has been written about the First World War than probably any other historical event. There are thousands of books covering every imaginable aspect of the

Here's an idea for you…

If you want to find out what your 'Daddy did in the Great War', be prepared to take time and persevere. Bear in mind, too, that this is probably one area of research where printed sources and the World Wide Web equal, if not outrank, manuscript sources in their ability to provide those sought-after facts.

conflict: you are certain to find several, if not a surfeit, of books covering any specific area of interest you may have. If you know little about the 'Great War' – its causes, course and aftermath – then initially the children's section of your local library or bookshop is a good starting point because the information is generally far clearer, objective and compact. Or look at the excellent websites designed for schools.

The Imperial War Museum in London is a rich source for information on many aspects of WWI. Although known principally as a 'museum', there are several departments holding a variety of information: personal documents, including unpublished diaries, poems, letters and memoirs; over six million photographs, including unit photographs, ships, hospitals and many individuals (although usually of senior personnel); film, video, and sound recording; and the collection of drawings and paintings commissioned under the official war artists scheme. Regimental museums and other specialist military repositories may also hold similar material

Defining idea…

'War is much too important a matter to be left to the generals.'
GEORGES CLEMENCEAU (1841–1929) French diplomat, poet and dramatist

to the Imperial War Museum, but related to their particular area of interest.

It is The National Archives (TNA) that holds nearly all the official records relating to the war itself, and those who fought in it. The three most important series of records are the Campaign Medal Rolls, the Official War Diaries and personnel Service Papers. These last are held at TNA only for those who left or were discharged in the years following the war: those who stayed on as career soldiers, sailors or airmen are still held by the Ministry of Defence.

Service records for army officers and ordinary soldiers have had very different histories since the end of the war. Those relating to officers who left the service before March 1922 have fared very well and, with only a few exceptions, all the papers survive. Unfortunately, for the enlisted men, the situation is quite different, as the majority of papers were destroyed or badly damaged by enemy action in 1940. In recent years, there has been a great deal of reconstruction work undertaken and now about 40% of papers for ordinary soldiers whose service ended before 1921 are available for research at TNA. These are in two series generally known as the 'burnt' and 'unburnt'.

How the Great War affected local communities was well covered by newspapers of the time, and the deaths of local 'boys' were also frequently included. See IDEA 9, *All the news that's fit to print*.

Try another idea...

'The first casualty when war comes is truth.'
HIRAM JOHNSON (1866–1945) US Senator

Defining idea...

Royal Navy officers (to 1920) and ordinary seamen (to 1928) also have a virtually completes series of service records. The Royal Air Force was founded on 1 April 1918, before which records of airmen will be found in either army (Royal Flying Corps) or naval records (Royal Naval Air Service). All those officers and airmen whose service included a period in the RAF (to 1920) have records held at TNA.

Campaign or war medals were awarded to members of the armed services for taking part in a campaign or for service in time of war. For the First World War, all servicemen of all services, some women, and some civilians, were eligible for one or more campaign medals if they served abroad. In addition to campaign medals, many other servicemen and women were awarded medals for gallantry or were mentioned in despatches. Again, all the records are held by TNA.

The War Diaries date from 1914 to 1922 and therefore cover the hostilities, and also the post-war armies of occupation. Some diaries record little more than daily losses, map references, etc.: others are much more descriptive. It is unusual for diaries to mention the names of ordinary soldiers, but you can sometimes find details in the diaries about awards of the Military Medal and the Meritorious Service Medal.

Discovering what somebody actually did, if they were in one of the Services, during the Great War (1914–1918) can be remarkably difficult. Service records, where they survive, give relatively little detail. Published and manuscript histories and diaries rarely give names, especially of those who were not officers. What is left is general information from which specific inferences have to be drawn.

Q **My grandfather was killed in action in about 1916. Will I be able to find out anything about him?**

How did it go?

A *Discovering information on those who died during the Great War, in any branch of the services as well as civilians and merchant seamen, is best commenced with the information held by the Commonwealth War Graves Commission. They have a really excellent website which includes rank and unit, date and place of death, and where they are buried or commemorated. Sometimes there is information about parents or spouse. Your grandfather's service records may also survive at TNA.*

Q **I've got no idea what role my grandfather might have played in the 1914–18 war because he and my grandmother both died young. What would be the best place for me start looking for information about his involvement?**

A *Because campaign medals were awarded to all servicemen and women, and anybody else who served overseas during the conflict, these records are the nearest we have to a full 'roll-call' for the First World War. Make the Campaign Medal Rolls at The National Archives your start point.*

26

For king and country

If not 'tinker or tailor' then possibly 'soldier or sailor'. In yesteryear, almost every family has been represented in its country's armed forces. Hence, a good place to look for ancestors.

Over the centuries many millions have joined the army or navy, or more recently the air forces, either as volunteers at times of their country's need or as career soldiers and sailors.

Before 1642, there was no regular standing army and the British Army per se can be said to date from the Restoration in 1660. Conscription was unnecessary until 1916, before which the British Army was made up entirely of volunteers. Part of the reason why this was so was that the need for men had historically been reasonably low. Even at the height of Britain's Imperial power, in the late nineteenth century, the numbers were surprisingly low: in 1899 there were only 180,000 serving officers and men.

Knowing where a regiment, or one of its battalions, was stationed at any particular date can be important; as can knowing what regiments were stationed at a particular place on a certain date. If it is known that a child was born in Gibraltar

Here's an idea for you... **Once you have determined the regiment – or sometimes regiments – an ancestor served in, then see if any regimental histories have been published. The regimental museum will hold copies, as may The National Archives' Library. Both the National Army Museum and Imperial War Museum's Libraries have important collections, as does the British Library.**

in 1872, then by discovering what regiments were there at that date, information on the father might be found using surviving army records. There are monthly returns that give the whereabouts of each regiment among the public records and a consolidated listing has been published.

The Imperial War Museum covers conflict from 1914 onwards. The National Army Museum is responsible for the earlier period, with material dating from 1485. The lives of ordinary soldiers are well illustrated, with letters, diaries, memoirs, and poems written by men stationed in every corner of the globe. These are supplemented by letter books, war diaries and order books, together with maps, records relating to several regiments, and over one million photographs.

But it is at The National Archives (TNA) that the majority of records relating to those who served in the British Army are to be found, both for officers and enlisted men. For the latter, these are almost exclusively for those discharged to pension and not for those who died in action, deserted or bought their way out. The records that do survive, from 1760, can be incredibly rewarding, often including considerable personal information as well as career details.

Defining idea... *'It is upon the navy, under the Providence of God, that the safety, honour, and welfare of this realm do chiefly attend.'*
CHARLES II (1630–1685)

For those who served in the Royal Navy, the records are again at TNA. For officers these are reasonably comprehensive from the Restoration. However, the situation for ratings is very different, as it was not until 1853 that any service records were kept by the Navy. Before that date, ordinary seamen did not join the 'Navy' but only individual ships for the lengths of their commissions – a few weeks or months, rarely longer than a year. It is difficult, usually impossible, to construct any service career for them and the ship's musters are one of the few place where information on ordinary seamen is to be found – though, to use these, the name of the ship(s) need(s) to be known.

> **If not fighting 'for king and country', there are other things your ancestors might have been doing. See IDEA 28, *Trades and occupations*, and IDEA 29, *Professions and professionals*.**
>
> Try another idea...

The constant threat of invasion and civil unrest meant that many men were members of the county militia regiments, yeomanries or sea fencibles. For the earlier years, the majority of the records relating to these men are to be found in county record offices; later records may also be held locally or are to be found at The National Archives.

The chances of anyone not having an ancestor who served in one of the armed forces is slim and the information that may be discovered, with a little perseverance, is considerable. And it may have been a 'family thing' with several generations serving in the army, navy or perhaps the Royal Marines, whose records too are to be found at TNA.

> **'The Battle of Waterloo was won on the playing fields of Eton.'**
>
> attributed to the DUKE OF WELLINGTON (1769–1852)
>
> Defining idea...

How did it go?

Q **I have been told that I have an ancestor who served at Waterloo. How can I find out if this is true?**

A *If all those who were said to have served at Waterloo were added up, the number would be many, many times the actual number who were really there. The same can be said for Trafalgar. There are no special or separate service records for those who fought at the great battles and for those discharged to pension; they will be among other service records. For all those discharged before 1855, the extant records have been indexed into TNA's online catalogue. So if you know this particular ancestor's name you can search this source. The first true British military campaign medal was awarded to all those who took part in the battles of Waterloo, Ligny and Quatre Bras, 16–18 June 1815, regardless of rank. Again, the records are at TNA.*

Q **I've just got a regimental history book for the cavalry brigade my father's Uncle Henry served in. Will I be able to find out much about him from there?**

A *Sadly, no. It's unlikely that your ancestor will be mentioned by name. However, a great deal of information will be given about the history of the regiment – where it went in the world and what battles and major national and international events it was involved in – and that could lead you in some more fruitful directions.*

27

Apprenticeship and apprentices

Apprenticeship indentures can be an invaluable source for discovering the origins of a tradesman or artisan among your ancestors.

Apprenticeship, as a means of training for work, has existed since time immemorial. Trade apprentices, charity apprentices or poor apprentices — nearly every trade required proper training for those who worked within it.

The Statute of Apprentices in 1563 forbade anyone from entering a trade who had not served an apprenticeship. Although modified over the centuries, it remained on the statute book until 1814. The Statute did not extend to trades that did not exist when it was passed in 1563. This therefore excluded many eighteenth-century industries, most notably the cotton industry. In many areas, the Statute was not enforced, and in the Yorkshire woollen industry, formal apprenticeship hardly existed by the end of the eighteenth century.

An apprentice would be bound to his master, or mistress, for a fixed period to learn his trade or craft, during which time he would usually be housed, fed and clothed at his master's expense. The apprentice undertook to obey certain rules relating to his conduct and was generally forbidden to marry until his apprenticeship was completed. All these conditions were laid out in a formal agreement, the apprenticeship indenture. Being personal agreements, few have survived unless among family papers. The rules relating to age and the term of apprenticeship varied a little over time, but essentially apprenticeship was for a seven-year period, ending at the age of 21. A general rule-of-thumb, therefore, is that most apprenticeships began when the child reached 14, although there are many exceptions to this.

Here's an idea for you...

Remember that many boroughs and cities had powerful guilds that regulated trade and apprenticeship and you can use their records to locate the craftsmen among your forebears. The London guilds and livery companies were among the most powerful and they produced extremely fine records, sometimes in unbroken series from the fourteenth century to the present day. Even when the formal apprenticeship system began to wane, craftsmen and tradesmen continued to become freemen of the companies and of the City itself. The records are now nearly all housed at Guildhall Library in the City.

There were three types of apprentice: trade, charity and poor. For those parents who could afford it, a trade and master were chosen, an indenture was prepared and a sum or premium was handed over. It was not until 1710 that there was any form of central registration of these trade apprenticeships and this was only brought about because the Commissioners of Stamps kept registers, until 1811, of the money they received from the duty on indentures. The records are held at The National Archives (TNA) and have been indexed, by both apprentices and masters, until 1774, by the Society of Genealogists. By the eighteenth century, apprenticeships were often undertaken without any formal indenture, especially in common trades such as weaving. In many trades it was expected that sons and nephews would be brought up in the same trade as their elders.

More information about what can be found in the 'parish chest' can be found at IDEA 30, *Get it off your chest*.

Try another idea...

For those parents who, although not paupers, could not afford to send their son or daughter to be apprenticed, there were numerous parish, local and county charities which were often able to help out. The records of these are mostly to be found at a local level, in county record offices or local archives covering the area where the family lived.

For the children of pauper families or those children who had no families (being orphans or illegitimate), it was the parish that saw to their well-being and arranged for their apprenticeship. Numerous Acts over the centuries, from the time of Elizabeth I, gave powers to the parish officials, the churchwardens and the overseers of the poor to put children out to apprenticeship.

Just as for the trade and charity apprentices, an indenture would be prepared. The second part of the document would be kept by the parish in the parish chest for safekeeping and very many survive to this day amongst a parish's records in the local county record office. However, poor or parish apprenticeships were exempt from tax and so no record appears in the 1710–1811 records at TNA.

The Dickensian view that all apprentices were ill-treated, starved and beaten is probably far from the truth. The purpose of apprenticeship was to produce the next generation of trades-

'The profession of a prostitute is the only career in which the maximum income is paid to the newest apprentice.'
WILLIAM BOOTH (1829-1912)

Defining idea...

'There is no worse apprentice than the one who doesn't want to know.'
Spanish proverb

men and craftsmen of the highest standard – then, just as now, it was realised that only by careful nurturing and good treatment (by their standards) would this be achieved. Many apprentices stayed on where they had been apprenticed, eventually marrying and raising families of their own.

Indentures can be an invaluable source for discovering where an ancestor came from or where they went, as well as adding more detail to their lives.

How did it go?

Q **An ancestor of mine is listed in the 1881 census as a boot- and shoemaker. He was born about 1855 and I would like to find out where he was apprenticed, and to whom. What are my chances?**

A *Try to find if his father or an uncle were also in the same trade, or even a much older brother. If that is the case then probably he was trained by one of them, without any formal apprenticeship. See if you can find him in the 1871 census because he may have been living in his master's home at the time.*

Q **Would the boys and girls have been apprenticed locally or might they have gone away somewhere?**

A *With parish apprentices, neither the children nor their parents had any real say in where the children were to be sent. They were often sent many miles from home and it was not until 1816 that a limit of forty miles was set.*

28

Trades and occupations

Were your ancestors higglers or badgers; labourers or lacemakers; clockmakers or carmen; or even working in the 'oldest profession'? Find out.

Ankle beater: A young person who helped to drive the cattle to market.

Back washer: A person employed to clean the wool in the worsted manufacturing industry.

Bagniokeeper: A person in charge of a bath house or brothel.

Tickney man or woman: A person who sold earthenware from town to town.

Knockknobbler: A dog catcher.

The names and meanings of obsolete occupations such as these have been lost in the mists of time as industrialisation and mechanisation brought massive changes to society. They have been replaced by occupations such as field sales manager, IT consultant, director at large, employee relations officer and animal psychologist.

Here's an idea for you... **Virtually every trade required proper training for those who worked within it, so look for the apprenticeship records for your forebears. Many archives contain details about the wheres, whens and hows for apprentices. Armed with the occupation of your ancestors, you could find fascinating new paths for your research.**

Some family historians spend a tremendous amount of time and effort locating their ancestors' birth, death and marriage details but pay little attention to what their ancestors actually did for a living. Just as we do today, our ancestors spent most of their waking hours working – be they rat catchers, watchmakers or brickmakers, they had to have a job to survive.

You might like to consider spending some time creating a through-life record for your ancestors, creating 'a picture' of their lives. You might want to discover why someone did a specific job, whether they had more than one job or if historical events affected their occupational choices. Along the way, you could also discover if their workplaces still exist or if they worked from home.

So, what were your ancestors' occupations? Bear in mind that it was often your ancestors themselves giving this information and, of course, it's all down to interpretation. Thus, an ancestor may describe himself simultaneously as a chimneysweep or labourer, or socially upgrade himself to become an artisan. It is not uncommon for some official records to require only the occupation of the head of the household, or the male, thus allowing a married women's occupation to be invisible.

To determine someone's occupation, try locating the record of their marriage or death, or the baptism or marriage of their children. Once you have ascertained an occupation, you can look at other records that can help you add to the information that you already have.

Census records survive from 1841 and they list the occupations of every adult in a household. You can check successive censuses (recorded every ten years) to see how occupations changed. Trade/city directories were compiled annually, and for large towns survive from the mid-eighteenth century, with county directories surviving from the early nineteenth century. These are also extremely useful, often listing the occupation in addition to the home address, allowing you to track people between the census years. Again, checking successive editions can show changes in an occupation. Copies of directories can be found in the local archive or online. Newspapers are another useful source – articles naming people usually give their occupation. Wills, probate records and military pension records can also provide valuable information.

A number of occupations were regulated by legislation. Some required a licence, sometimes to ensure adequate competence (as in the case of gamekeepers) or to ensure that the law was obeyed (such as for victuallers). These records can often be found among the Quarter Sessions records at local archives.

Surviving employment records should be found at the relevant local archives where the business was based. There are a number of museums and dedicated archives covering specific occupations while others hold specialist collections, such as those relating to trade union records.

Once you have a full career record for any ancestors, you can begin to intertwine it with their day-to-day life events and the wider history

The provision of free education was a phenomenon of the late 1800s and the push for social reform. To discover if your ancestor had any formal education, look at IDEA 12, Reading, 'riting, 'rithmetic.

Try another idea...

'We have not all had the good fortune to be ladies. We have not all been generals, or poets, or statesmen; but when the toast works down to the babies, we stand on common ground.'
MARK TWAIN (1835–1910)

Defining idea...

unfolding around them. This will help you to determine why they had that occupation and what made them the way they were. It really can bring the individuals to life.

How did it go?

Q How do I find the meaning of a specific occupation?

A *The meanings of the more commonly known occupations can be found in an ordinary dictionary. For information on more obsolete terms, consult one of the original dictionaries dating from the eighteenth or nineteenth centuries – they can be found in your local archive or at the British Library. It is also worth searching the internet because there is quite a lot to be found online and there are also some occupation-related mailing lists that you can subscribe to. In addition, numerous specialist publications have been produced that list unusual occupations and are aimed at local and family historians. Some of them include facsimiles of old books. There are also a number of books about researching specific occupations, be it midwives or publicans. Many of these are available to purchase or can be found through your local library.*

Q So why might someone have more than one job or trade?

A *Apart from soldiers or sailors, who would also have had a civilian trade, many other people had trades that complemented each other, such as printer and publisher, auctioneer and valuer, carpenter and joiner – many of which have survived to the present day. A lot of other dual occupations were seasonal, such as farm labourer during the summer months and brewery worker in the winter. These seasonal occupations may be missed from a census return but can be discovered through the sources already discussed or by delving into the local history of an area.*

29

Professions and professionals

Architects, doctors, clerics, surgeons, MPs, lawyers, dentists and their ilk: professionals are usually far easier to trace than ancestors who were labourers.

The majority of professions have been regulated by organisations, which have granted qualifications, governed the professionals in their good practice, and kept those all-important records.

It is worth contacting the governing body of any profession to see what records exist and which of them might include information on your forebears. A search of the internet will almost certainly take you to the website of the organisation, which itself may cover the information you want, as well as how to access the material.

Here's an idea for you...

It is often very useful to know what was entailed in any profession – or trade or other occupation for that matter – and there are very many books available. These range from relatively cheap books in the Shire Publications series to weighty tomes produced by academics. Usually the former are sufficient to give a good background and often include illustrations that enhance the text and bring the past to life. Understanding the past often comes from an appreciation of what our ancestors actually did, day to day; what it entailed and what this meant for their own lives and those of their families. Many professionals and others kept diaries of their lives and what their work involved. See if you can find anything for the relevant time and occupation of your ancestors.

You should find in your local reference library *British Archives: A Guide to Archive Resources in the United Kingdom*, which will also give you the contact details and some indication of what is held by the relevant organisation. The *Aslib Directory of Information Sources in the UK* is also a useful reference book to be found in your reference library.

These governing bodies frequently published registers or yearbooks giving the names and qualifications of their members, plus the address at which they practised. For medics, there is *The Medical Register* and *The Medical Directory*; for lawyers there is *The Law List*; for dentists, *The Dentists Register*; and for church-men, the *Clergy List* and *Crockfords' The Clerical Directory*. There are many, many others – for veterinary surgeons, nurses, architects, teachers and so forth.

Over the years, many cumulative lists of professionals have been produced, under their chosen career, by interested individuals or a related organisation. Again, these are going to be found in specialist libraries, such as that of the Society of Genealogists in London. There are lists like *Eighteenth Century Medics*, covering apothecaries and barber-surgeons as well as doctors and surgeons; or *Men at the Bar*, compiled by Joseph Foster back in 1885; or his *Index Ecclesiasticus* covering the period 1800 to 1840. Many published works cover specific places (e.g. something like Norfolk Clergy).

Not a doctor or a lawyer, but a 'haggler' or an 'ag. lab.'? Then try IDEA 28, *Trades and occupations*.

Try another idea...

Many professionals, particularly clerics, attended university. Before 1832 in England, this meant Oxford or Cambridge – the others were Trinity in Dublin and St Andrews in Scotland. All these universities have published lists of alumni, which often include details of the careers of the former students after they left the university in question as well as details of parents and siblings who also attended the university.

Detailed biographies of many of the more eminent professionals can be found in the *Oxford Dictionary of National Biography*, which is available in book form and online in some of the larger libraries. For many professions there are specific biographical

'A professional is a man who can do his best at a time when he doesn't particularly feel like it.'
ALISTAIR COOKE (1908–2005)
English-US broadcaster journalist

Defining idea...

works, but these are only likely to be found in specialist libraries or at the British Library.

Those from the professions are more likely to have left wills than others and this can be a useful source for family details, possibly used in conjunction with the Victorian census returns. And they are also likely to appear in the trade directories from the early and mid-nineteenth century. In fact, the earliest directories were lists of professionals, such as surgeons and lawyers, together with the major tradesmen in the City of London.

Actors and other entertainers are usually difficult to research because they went through no formal training and moved around the country a great deal. However, again, there are many biographical works available, as well as contemporary newspapers and magazines, such as *The Era*, which was published from 1838. The Theatre Museum in Covent Garden is a goldmine of information, with thousands of photographs and over a million playbills and programmes.

Professional ancestors may be easier to trace because of the many specialist sources available, but a profession was, and is, simply another occupation and professionals were treated no different when it came to registering the births of their children or being recorded in the census.

Q **The family I am researching all seem to have been labourers and the like. Suddenly I have found one in a census described as a 'lawyer'. Can this be right? How can I find out more?**

How did it go?

A *This is probably one of the most common errors to be made when reading some census entries, and even birth, marriage and death certificates. Your ancestor was probably a 'sawyer' not a 'lawyer'. The two letters, L and S, are frequently indistinguishable; so have another closer look at the entry. Another thing to watch out for is exaggeration. Many an agricultural labourer appears as a farmer at his death. Even the most humble get themselves entered as 'gentleman' occasionally. Soldiers become officers and potmen become licensed victuallers.*

Q **My dad says mum's mum was in the 'oldest profession'. What is that?**

A *Ask your mother. On second thoughts, no, best not! There are some parts of your family history you may need to tip-toe carefully around.*

30

Get it off your chest

Parish chests are a rich supply of information rarely found anywhere else. They can give you a fantastic insight into the life of your forebears.

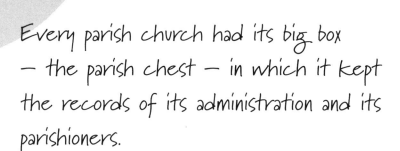

Every parish church had its big box — the parish chest — in which it kept the records of its administration and its parishioners.

The 1552 Poor Law directed every parish to provide a strong chest, having three keys, for holding the alms for the poor. From the early sixteenth century, separate legislation required that every parish should have a locking chest to contain the parish registers and all other documents pertaining to the parish. Often only one chest was provided and was adapted to serve both purposes.

Over the centuries, various acts of parliament increased parish responsibilities, which meant that, prior to the nineteenth century, the parish church was the centre for both religious and civil administration in the parish. This resulted in various documents connected with the running of the parish being stored in the parish chest along with the church silver and communion plate.

Many other officials associated with the parish besides the clergy generated records useful to the family and local historian. Churchwardens' records cover a wide range of expenditure, including payments to the poor and details of bastardy. The parish was reluctant to accept financial responsibility for an unmarried mother with child so they went to great lengths to discover the identity of the father and ensure that he was made financially responsible, much as the Child Support Agency tries to do today. Minutes of vestry meetings held to discuss parish business usually survive from the eighteenth century onwards. The vestry could also levy rates for such things as the maintenance of the highways, poor relief and the care of maimed soldiers and vagrants, and was also responsible for appointing the parish constable and other officers.

The parish constable had the power of arrest and brought prisoners before the local magistrate. Constables' accounts and vouchers should be sought for details of payments relating to this. From 1757, the parish was responsible for compiling lists of men to serve in the 'militia', and many of these lists have survived. The parish also maintained public roads, so the Accounts of the Surveyors of Highways, which recorded expenditure and payments received, can be a valuable source for family historians.

Overseers' Accounts give names and details of payments for rent, clothes, medical and funeral expenses for the poor. Poor Rate Books contain details of those who paid rates and are a useful census substitute for the more prosperous parishioners.

Here's an idea for you… **Check if there is a local history society or someone undertaking a one-place study covering your parish of interest, and tap into this fantastic source of 'local' knowledge.**

Other records found within the parish chest relate to settlement and removal. Completing a parish apprenticeship was a way of obtaining legal settlement in a parish. Where parents could pay, a child would be apprenticed by voluntary consent. However, where pauper children were concerned, the parish officers could compel parishioners to take them as apprentices.

Besides acting as secretary to the vicar, the parish clerk's duties included collecting fees, leading the responses during church services and ringing the bells. Some ministers and parish officers treated their registers and the various account books almost like diaries, including information about the weather, harvests, local gossip and other local events. Other documents surviving may include copies of taxation returns, confirmation lists, parish magazines, mortgages, maps and parish plans. Another important source are the Glebe Terriers – records of church lands and property. These often mentioned the tenants or owners of the adjoining as well as church lands, and along with tithe maps are useful in pinpointing exactly where an ancestor lived.

Survival of these records depends not only on the local mouse population but also on the extent to which the church officer's housekeeping zeal led to old 'rubbish' being discarded. Where they exist, these records can be usually be found in the local diocesan (county) record office or, occasionally, in private hands or archives.

As you gather more information about your family it is very important to organise your research properly, following the golden rules of Clarity, Convenience and Completeness. For more tips on achieving this, see IDEA 19, *Files, formats and family trees.*

Try another idea…

'It matters not how a man dies, but how he lives. The act of dying is not of importance, it lasts so short a time.'
SAMUEL JOHNSON (1709–1784)
lexicographer, critic and poet

Defining idea…

How did
it go?

Q   How were churchwardens appointed, what did they actually do and what records did they generate that could help us?

A   *Churchwardens, or guardians of the parish church, were elected each Easter for the year by the vicar and parishioners, or the vestry (governing body of the parish). Churchwardens undertook a number of duties, including managing church property and income, administration of parish charities, upkeep of the church, allocating pews (for payment), maintaining the parish registers, and arranging the burials of strangers and baptisms of foundlings. They could also summon parishioners to attend church courts – for failing to attend church, libel or blasphemy.*

Q   I have seen references to removal orders and settlement. What do these signify?

A   *From 1691, settlement (legal residence) could be gained by birth in a parish, by various rent or rate qualifications, by being apprenticed to a parishioner or by serving a year as a parish officer. Anyone who wished to relocate from one parish to another needed to obtain a certificate confirming that his parish of settlement would take responsibility if he needed poor relief. Overseers of the poor had the power to have a pauper examined by the local justice of the peace and removed back to his home parish. Records generated include 'settlement examinations' and 'removal orders'. Where settlement was granted, the individuals and their families could apply for a 'settlement certificate' to enable them to work and settle outside their home parishes. The system died out in the early nineteenth century.*

31

Arms and the man

Heraldry is all around us – on inn signs, in stained-glass church windows and as hatchments (armorial bearings of the dead) – and perhaps on the spoons in your cutlery drawer.

Personal and civic heraldry have been with us for the greater part of the last millennium. Get your crayons out – it's colouring-in time.

Imagine a football match with all the players wearing the same coloured strip. Not only would the referee get in a complete mess but the teams themselves wouldn't know which players were theirs and which weren't. It was the same in medieval times when it was necessary in battle to be able to distinguish between friend and foe: before the introduction of distinctive colours and badges for the opposing sides, there was frequently great confusion and many a disaster.

Initially, brightly coloured banners were used for identification, often with some form of emblem. This idea extended itself to shields and then to surcoats worn over chain mail (hence the term coat-of-arms). With the advent of tournaments as popular forms of entertainment, armour became much more elaborate and the emblem or 'device' was extended to the liveries worn by servants and members of the household.

As heraldry flourished and became regulated by the College of Arms in London – as it still is – it became necessary to introduce a language whereby a herald could accurately describe arms. The language used was Norman-French – as it is to this day. The simplest arms are usually the oldest, and those with no crest or motto probably date from before the fifteenth century. More recent grants of arms tend to feature elements that associate the bearer with his or her career. For instance, Lord Zuckerman's arms pay tribute to his work for London Zoo and so feature a gorilla; Elton John's arms incorporate a keyboard.

'Reading' a coat-of-arms may look totally impossible, but you can easily break it down into a number of parts, each with its own purpose and meaning. There are plenty of books around that go into the fine detail. A 'complete achievement' consists of a shield of arms, usually with the addition of a crest born on a helmet, and frequently with a motto below. The crest was originally there to ward off blows to the head and often took the form of a device fashioned out of boiled leather. Fabulous birds, beasts and inanimate objects, such as ships and castles, were all popular.

Attached to the helmet is the mantling, which resembles and derives from the material used to protect the helmet and the head from the extreme heat of the sun encountered in the Crusades. Supporters, usually found in pairs on either side of the shield, are restricted to

Here's an idea for you...

Turn your next pub crawl into an heraldic adventure by only visiting those hostelries named after coats-of-arms or badges or other elements taken from the world of heraldry: The King's Arms, The White Hart, The Bear and Ragged Staff, The Feathers, The Wheatsheaf etc. Then see if you can find out why the pub is called what it is. For example, the Bear and Ragged Staff represents the Earl of Warwick; the Feathers, the Black Prince. The Wheatsheaf stands for bakers and Horseshoes for blacksmiths.

the more illustrious achievements and to civic arms.

The shield itself is where the 'shorthand for history' is to be found. As armigerous families intermarried, so the shields became divided and quartered (any number of even parts, not just four) according to strict rules. And so the simplest of arms could evolve, becoming more and more complicated over time, but encompassing the history of the family.

The motto has far more obscure origins. In some cases it may have derived from an ancient battle cry but it may relate to a more important happening in the history of the family, a religious bias, or even simply a pun on the name. The Barnard family, whose arms depict a black bear with a gold muzzle ('argent a bear rampant sable muzzled or'), uses the motto 'Bear and Forbear'.

Civic heraldry, which is connected with towns and cities, usually tells something of their history or connection with a particular family. For example, in the arms of Birmingham, two of the most prominent families are represented: the de Bermingham family by gold lozenges; and the Calthorpe family by an ermine fess (bar).

The heraldry all around us is far more than just decoration. Once interpreted, the origin and meaning of any particular coat-of-arms can expand the knowledge and understanding of both family and local history.

Tombstones, and particularly the more elaborate edifices commemorating whole families, frequently include the arms if the family was armigerous. Read IDEA 11, *Writ in Stone*, and get investigating.

Try another idea…

'The boast of heraldry, the pomp of power,
And all that beauty, all that wealth e'er gave,
Awaits alike th' inevitable hour.
The paths of glory lead but to the grave.'
THOMAS GRAY (1716–1771) Elegy written in a country churchyard

Defining idea…

**Q   My name is Hewitt, which I have discovered is the family name
of the Earls of Lifford. I have also found out that there are several Hewitt arms, all slightly different. Which one can I use?**

A   *Probably none of them. If your family ever was entitled to a coat-of-arms
then it is very unlikely that this is something that would be forgotten by
the generations. It is enormously important to remember that arms belong
to a family and not to a name.*

**Q   I've seen people selling coats-of-arms and name origins. Are
they likely to have the correct one for me?**

A   *There are lots of companies that will sell you computer printouts of coats-
of-arms just based on your surname. They can look great on the wall of the
smallest room, but don't rush off and have your stationery reprinted or get
a seal made until you have proved these belong to your family as well.*

32

Manors maketh man

Lords and labourers all contributed to the extraordinary records of the manorial courts, which can reveal the history of communities from the twelfth century.

Manorial documents are among the few types of records where genealogical information about ordinary people — rather than the upper classes — is likely to survive from medieval times.

The manor was at the centre of feudal society and was essentially the government of the local community in medieval times. It not only had administrative control but also functioned as a court of law for minor, and some not so minor, offences. The owner of the manor, the Lord, was answerable to the King. Everyone had their roles within a strict order and it was extremely difficult to rise above those positions.

Within the manor, land could be held in several ways. The first was by '*customary tenure*' – that is, by tradition in return for working on the Lord's own land. The descent of these holdings was governed by 'custom', or accepted rules of the manor

The difficulties of using manorial documents include the handwriting and language, which in medieval times was Latin. English became more common in Tudor times, but many manorial court records continued in Latin until the eighteenth century. To unravel these records, check out two online tutorials – one on palaeography (old handwriting) and one on Latin – produced by The National Archives. These are really user-friendly and even for the absolute novice are an excellent idea.

in question. The commonest form of customary tenure was known as '*copyhold* tenure', because each tenant was given a copy of the entry in the manor court roll that recorded his succession.

Freehold land was usually held in return for a fixed rent. Its descent was not governed by the manor but freeholders were still subject to manorial jurisdiction in other respects, so that they do also appear in the records. Others held *leasehold* land. Over the centuries the authority of the Lord of the Manor was reduced, although the last vestiges of the copyhold system survived until 1922.

The records of the lords of the manor and the manorial courts still exist and in some places go back centuries, from the present day back to well before the commencement of parish records. The area governed by a manor court was usually quite different to the parish's area: any one manor may have within its boundary the whole or parts of one or more parishes, and vice versa.

Defining idea...

'If a man owns land, the land owns him.'
RALPH WALDO EMERSON (1803–1882) American essayist, poet and philosopher

There were two main types of manorial court, both of which produced comprehensive records of their meetings. The Court Leet dealt with minor offences, such as straying cattle, ditches not being cleared, hedges not being maintained or selling underweight goods (and even with more serious offences in earlier times).

The most useful manorial records are those generated by the *Court Baron*, which met several times each year. This business would include the reporting of tenants' deaths – in theory, freehold as well as customary tenants – and the payment to the Lord of the corresponding feudal due, a fine or *heriot*. When the heir of a dead customary tenant succeeded, the *'surrender'* of the land and the *'admission'* of the new tenant would be recorded, the relationship between the two usually being noted. Occasionally, there are payments noted for the marriages of the daughters of customary tenants or records of the remarriage of widows. Other tenants will be named in the records: as officials or jurors, they may be noted as absent, or they may be fined, *'amerced'*, for some minor offence.

Another important record is the Manorial *Survey*. Over time, these assumed different forms: usually they include at least a list of the names of the manorial tenants, and may give much fuller information. The *'custumal'*, common in the twelfth and thirteenth centuries, recorded the tenants, their holdings and their obligations to the lord; the *'extent'*, a valuation of the manor; and the *'rental'*, which listed tenants and the rents payable. Occasionally a plan of the manorial extents exists that is associated with the rental.

Most manorial records are private, not public, and so their survival has been more a matter of luck than of routine. Large numbers of medieval documents have been lost. For known surviving records, and their location, there is an official listing – the Manorial Docu-

Manorial records are ideally used together with contemporary maps and plans. See IDEA 17, *How does the land lie?*

Try another idea…

'You had better have a rich landlord … you will find that every man is worse for being poor.'

GEORGE BERNARD SHAW
(1856–1950)

Defining idea…

ments Register – held at The National Archives (TNA). For a few counties only, the listing is available online. Most court records will be found in the county record office, but many are still in private hands or even overseas. TNA has a large collection of records for Crown manors.

Manor court records can reveal much about our ancestors' lives. Looking through these documents, it is possible to trace the changes in land holdings, which can be the only record in earlier times of deaths, marriage and inheritance.

How did it go?

Q   I have managed to locate where some manorial records are held. Is there anything useful I can read before going to see them?

A   A volume in the Victoria County History *series might help. This could tell you which families were Lords of the Manor and give you other useful information. Your local reference library may have a complete set of the VCH.*

Q   Some of the records I have found seem to be held in a record office for a completely different county. Why might this be?

A   Many Lords, particularly in more recent centuries, had their 'seat' far away from the manors they owned; hence, the documentation can be far removed from the place it refers to. This is why the Manorial Documents Register is so important.

33

Crime and punishment

**For the family historian, crime really does pay. Criminal
ancestors left an extensive paper trail, allowing you
to uncover a tremendous amount of information about
them.**

*Your ancestors would, of course, never
have been involved in anything really nasty
— or would they? Perhaps so but I expect it's
much more likely they were the victims.*

There is an extremely good chance that one of your ancestors has appeared in the
criminal courts either as defendant, plaintiff, victim, witness or even as a member
of the jury, so legal records are well worth looking into.

Punishments included the use of the pillory, stocks, ducking stool, carting, whipping,
fines and, for debtors particularly, prison. The greatest change in punishment, however, was the introduction of transportation to the American colonies in the 1660s.

The death penalty was extensively used as a punishment and by 1688 fifty crimes
were punishable by death, rising by 1815 to over 225. Capital offences included
murder, treason, counterfeiting, arson, stealing horses or sheep, destroying turn-
pike roads, cutting down growing trees, pick-pocketing goods worth more than 1

Here's an idea for you...

Reasons for crime were as hotly discussed in the past as they are today. Once you have located the details of a specific court case, trawl through the local newspapers to see if they contain any additional information such as eyewitness reports of the offence.

shilling, being out at night with a blackened face, deliberately breaking tools used in the manufacture of wool or stealing from a rabbit warren. The idea was that punishment should be as harsh a deterrent as possible. By 1841 only murder and treason remained as capital crimes, the others having been abolished.

Prior to 1800, imprisonment was rarely used as a punishment, prisons being mainly places where individuals were held for trial or until their sentences were implemented. The group of people who were the exception were debtors, who could be imprisoned until their debt was paid.

From the fourteenth century, Justices of the Peace (JPs) held their own courts four times a year. These were known as Quarter Sessions and they were a vital part of the legal system, taking over much of the work of the Royal Judges. JPs dealt with all kinds of cases, from murder, poaching, vagrancy and assault to whether local landowners were paying their workers the going rate. These records also cover such matters as: by-law offences, licensing offences, non-payment of tithes and taxes, non-payment under bastardy orders, apprenticeship offences, Poor Law offences and many of the same crimes as the Assize Courts. JPs were usually wealthy land-owners and until recent times had no legal training. Nevertheless they were able to impose sentences of death or transportation.

Records of the Quarter Sessions and the Petty Sessions can survive from the six-teenth century. They are usually found in the local County Record Office. However, a detailed listing of the whereabouts of the surviving records has been published. The details are on the Access to Archives website – www.a2a.org.uk

Begin your prowl and discover what's found where within the giant labyrinth of archives, libraries and record repositories. Try IDEA 18, *Become a where wolf.*

Try another idea…

Criminal records are to be found divided between The National Archives (TNA) and local record offices. The National Archives holds the records for the higher or more important criminal courts, which includes the Assize Courts, the Central Criminal Court (the Old Bailey) plus the Exchequer and Chancery courts, which tried important civil cases. Records relating to bankruptcy and debt can also be found at TNA. The records of the original Old Bailey sessions (1673–1834) are available online and fully searchable. They make extremely interesting reading.

Family historians who take the time to research these types of legal documents will often be pleasantly surprised by the rewards that are in store. The amount of information contained within a court file can vary greatly from one case to another and from one region of the country to another. In general, you should hope to find dates and places of births, marriages, and deaths; the names and ages of children; information about your relatives' residences; and financial and employment information.

The records are not always easy to read, but sometimes the material they contain is pure gold, with the trial details providing a fascinating insight into our ancestors' lives and the world they lived in. In addition, they'll allow you to discover if you are descended from a sinner or a saint.

'If you can't get rid of the skeleton in your closet, you'd best teach it to dance.'
GEORGE BERNARD SHAW
(1856–1950)

Defining idea…

How did
it go?

Q   How do I find out about my police officer ancestor?

A   *Prior to the nineteenth century, policing was carried out locally by watch-men, constables and magistrates. The records created are usually found in local record offices. The first modern police force was the London Metro-politan Police force, established in 1829, with provincial county forces com-mencing after the County Police Act of 1839. The records of these modern forces are either retained by the police themselves or deposited at the appropriate record office. The National Archives holds the records for the London Metropolitan Police force and the Royal Irish Constabulary.*

Q   There is a family story that an ancestor was transported. How do I find more information?

A   *From the seventeenth century, royal pardons were granted to many condemned convicts, on condition that they were transported to work on plantations in the American colonies. Usually the sentences were for seven or fourteen years but many were transported for life. In all, 56,000 people were transported. Transportation ceased on the outbreak of the American Revolutionary War in 1776. Lists of references to convicts transported to America have been indexed and published. Transportation resumed in 1787 with a new destination: Australia. By 1830, it was becoming very expen-sive and the end of transportation to New South Wales finally came after the discovery of gold and the resulting gold rush of 1851. A further 9,500 convicts were sent to Western Australia between 1850 and 1868, when the transportation system finally ended. Many of these records have been indexed.*

34

Let's get out of here

Emigration has generated a wide diversity of records, which, due to their very origins, need to be hunted for in a number of different places.

The grass has always been greener somewhere else. And if the somewhere else was another country or colony, then emigration resulted. Single members to extended families all sought a better life away from the mother country.

Over the centuries, one of Britain's most prolific exports has been its people. This has taken many guises, be it voluntarily, to travel the world, to explore, seek fame and fortune, to trade, to colonise and govern; or forcibly, through transportation, to fight or to garrison some far-off settlement.

When trying to trace the origins of someone who emigrated from the British Isles, you should begin by using all the sources that are available in the country to which they went in order to locate just where in the British Isles your emigrant ancestor

Take a look in the local newspapers covering the areas where your ancestors lived. Obituaries of emigrant ancestors can cover in surprising detail all aspects of their lives, including the names of relatives in the old country and occasionally place of birth.

hailed from. There are very few passenger lists of people leaving the British Isles prior to the nineteenth century – arrival in the foreign country is more likely to have been recorded than departure from the British Isles.

Published records relating to early emigrants to the West Indies, American colonies, Australia and New Zealand can be found but, as always, it is important that you also check the original source material because it may contain extra information. Merchants and travellers abroad may also be located among records at The National Archives. Much, of course, can also be found on the internet.

The Society of Genealogists (London) holds one of the best collections of printed material relating to emigration and the Church of Jesus Christ of Latter-day Saints maintains considerable collections of lists compiled from sources worldwide.

You can uncover details of many births, marriages and deaths of passengers at sea, and of Britons abroad (which were registered at British consulates, embassies and legations) in sources held at The National Archives and the Family Records Centre. However, there is no overall index to them, and they are not complete. They generally start from the beginning of the nineteenth century and at least allow you to discover where people were at a given date, thus opening the doors to other contemporary sources for more information.

There are a number of sources that can provide information on the emigration experience. For example, the government set regulations for its local agents when selecting emigrants for free passages to New South Wales, Western Australia, Tasmania and New Zealand. The regulations set out what bedding was provided for emigrants, what clothing it was expected they would need for the voyage and what trade tools they could take. You can also occasionally find references to payments covering emigrants' travel expenses to their port of embarkation in parish records.

Slabs, brasses, headstones, memorials, crematoria and churchyards can all bring the dead back to life, even giving a hint to a place of birth. Look at IDEA 11, *Writ in stone*.

Try another idea…

Research studies into emigration now acknowledge the important role played by newspapers and the notices they carried, particularly in providing information about the means of emigration – information about the departure and arrival of ships and advertisements giving the names of local agents through whom passages might be arranged are all listed. These newspapers also carried details of land that was available to purchase by prospective immigrants.

A more sophisticated means of drawing attention to the mechanics of emigration were perhaps the published letters that also appeared in the newspapers – particularly from the early 1770s, a period of increased emigration mainly in reaction to depressed circumstances affecting the linen industry and trade. These were letters ostensibly written by passengers who had made the crossing and whose first thought on arrival was apparently to write to the newspaper. The stories they told of relative success and, above all perhaps, satisfaction with their initial decision to make the move, must have provided the reassurance that intending emigrants wanted to hear.

'All travel has its advantages. If the passenger visits better countries, he may learn to improve his own. And if fortune carries him to worse, he may learn to enjoy it.'
SAMUEL JOHNSON (1709–1784)
lexicographer, critic and poet

Defining idea…

155

How did it go?

Q   Where can I find information on child emigration?

A   It is thought that between 1618 and 1967, 150,000 children were sent to America, Australia, Canada, Rhodesia, New Zealand, South Africa and the Caribbean. Many of the children were in the care of the voluntary organisations that arranged for their migration. Later schemes were sponsored by the destination country. Where they exist, the records can best be located in the countries of destination.

Q   Do passport records survive?

A   Passports only became compulsory in 1915. Prior to that they were mainly issued to businessmen, merchants or diplomats. There was no requirement to have a passport to emigrate to a British colony, or to enter the USA. There were, however, restrictions on British subjects travelling abroad and 'licences to pass beyond the seas' had to be obtained until the eighteenth century. Registers of oaths of allegiance taken before departing, and of the licences issued, can be found at The National Archives. These include lists of soldiers taking the oath prior to going to fight overseas. Until 1858, UK passports could be granted to people who were not British but required the protection of the UK while travelling. These requested that the holder be allowed to travel without hindrance. Many European countries used passports during the First World War as a form of ID. If you have old passports within the family archive, they can provide quite a lot of useful information, although records relating to issue of the passports actually contain very little.

35

Aliens in the family

Your ancestors may have been among the refugees, merchants and entrepreneurs who, over the centuries, decided that the grass was greener in Britain and made the move.

From time immemorial, individuals and families from overseas relocated to the British Isles to find work, escape from religious or political persecution, or simply seek a better life.

Some immigrants stayed in Britain for only a short time, either soon going back home or moving on again, while others made it their permanent home. Geography has always made England a natural destination for emigrants from the continent of Europe. Immigration during recent years tends to make people forget that the earliest immigrants came not as refugees but were usually invited to come by the Crown or government of the day. From as far back as Henry I in 1113, immigrants were offered asylum for both altruistic and selfish reasons, knowing that the country would benefit from their knowledge and skills.

After Henry VIII split from the Church of Rome, England became a place of exile for Protestants fleeing persecution in Europe. These included French Protestants

Here's an idea for you...

If you've any interest in migration to the UK, discover *Moving Here* (www. movinghere.org.uk), a website that focuses on the experiences of the Jewish (from Eastern Europe), Irish and people from the Caribbean and South Asia from the 1840s to the present day. Also included is information on how you can use these resources for your own research. This website offers free access, for personal and educational use, to online versions of original material related to migration, including photographs, personal papers, government documents, maps and art objects, as well as a collection of sound recordings and video clips.

Defining idea...

'Immigrant, n. An unenlightened person who thinks one country better than another.'
     AMBROSE BIERCE (1842–?1914),
               The Devil's Dictionary

from as early as the sixteenth century, and especially the Huguenots and Walloons from the late seventeenth century, plus exiles from the Palatinate in the early eighteenth century. During the eighteenth and nineteenth centuries, further Protestant refugees flooded into Britain, notably those fleeing from the French Revolution in 1789. There were no controls on immigration into England until the beginning of the war with France in 1793.

During the nineteenth century, unemployment and overpopulation in Ireland resulted in many labourers coming to England to find work, particularly between 1815 and 1830. Famine in Ireland between 1845 and 1851 caused thousands more to emigrate to England and Scotland, and, of course, to the United States.

Italians arrived from the early nineteenth century, congregating around Clerkenwell in London, and later spreading into Soho. The first settlers were craftsmen and precision instrument makers, as well those as bringing Italian ice-cream to the British.

In 1290, Edward I had expelled all Jews from England, and they were not readmitted until the Commonwealth under Cromwell, in 1656. Russian and Polish Jews began to arrive in the last two decades of the nineteenth century and then again during the periods of Jewish persecution leading up to the Second World War.

Family photographs may include clues to origins of immigrant ancestors. For more, see IDEA 46, *Families in Focus*.

Try another idea…

Following the 1948 British Nationality Act, there began the first major immigration of West Indians in large numbers to their 'mother country'.

At an early date, it became necessary to introduce a procedure for admitting foreigners to all or some of the privileges of a natural-born British subject. Before 1844, there were two methods of obtaining the privileges of a native: (1) by taking out an 'act of naturalisation', or (2) by 'letters of denization'. The most important difference was that in the case of denization the privileges conveyed were not retrospective but commenced only from the date of the grant – aliens were not entitled to hold land in the country, and letters of denization were not sufficient to enable a man to inherit, nor confer any benefit on children born previous to the date of the grant.

The records of denization and naturalisation, which date from about 1400, are to be found mainly at The National Archives (TNA). There are, fortunately, combined indexes to all the classes and collections of records concerned. In particular, all naturalisations from 1844 to 1936 are indexed into TNA's online 'Catalogue'. Even so, the records held at TNA are sparse and difficult to use. Lists of ships' passengers entering from abroad survive in the public records from 1890 to 1960 but they are only for vessels sailing from places outside Europe. There are no comparable lists or registers concerned with people arriving in the UK by air.

'Immigration is the sincerest form of flattery.'
JACK PAAR (1918–2004)
American talk-show host and comedian

Defining idea…

Discovering you have an immigrant family in your past should come as no surprise – most of us do. With luck and perseverance your research may take you to another country and the records held there. It is sure to raise the question: 'Why did they come to the UK?'

How did it go? **Q** **I have found a branch of my family in the census returns, but it just says they were 'born in Prussia'. Will I be able to find their whereabouts in Prussia? And where was Prussia anyway?**

A *Prussia was a north German state stretching eastwards from the Low Countries out along the Baltic coast into current-day Poland. It was dissolved in 1947, following the Second World War. To track your relatives, try looking for specific locations in the records of naturalisation at The National Archives, and keep an eye out for any possible brothers or uncles too. Also, the Anglo-German Family History Society might be able to help you.*

Q **I have a similar problem, as the census returns just give 'born in Ireland'.**

A *As all of Ireland was part of Great Britain until 1922, there will be no naturalisation records to help. So, make sure you check all the available census returns because one of them might include the town in Ireland where they were born. It's no consolation, but the surviving returns for Ireland similarly only state 'England' for place of birth.*

36

Helical help

Not too long ago, you were the child of your father according to your mother. Today, genetics can help in determining our origins, but it's still not the great revealer that many believe.

Any undesirable traits in our children came from their other parent.

If the main reason why we research our past is to discover who we are, then it is not surprising that the implications of genetic research have become a fascination among many family historians in recent years. The fact that genetics may help prove, or disprove, who our ancestors are, or indicate that disparate family groups with the same surname do in fact all descend from the same pair of ancestors, is only part of this new area of interest. That we may now be able to know which of our traits and characteristics were passed on to us by ancestors now gone is an interesting prospect. And that we can now seriously consider what we might pass on to future generations could be a matter of considerable importance. At least, that is the theory.

According to one expert: 'Knowing our genetic profiles can help us fulfil our desires to add lasting meaning to human life.' However, that is probably doubtful. Nevertheless, many family historians are expanding their research to create family health histories that may point to disease-causing genes in their families.

Here's an idea for you... **Look on the internet and you will find several firms advertising that they will undertake Ycs or mtDNA tests (or both) for a few hundred pounds. You can even receive a 'Y-Line certificate, suitable for framing'. However, using DNA to help trace your ancestry is currently not something that most will be able to take advantage of. Where it is already becoming of use is in confirming, or otherwise, that families living in different parts of the country, or in different countries around the world, and having the same or similar surname, do have a common ancestor.**

Now for the science. Our bodies are made up of basic building blocks called cells. Each cell has a nucleus, which controls the cell's functions. Within the nucleus are two sets of chromosomes, 23 received from the mother and 23 from the father. Each chromosome is comprised of strings of DNA (deoxyribonucleic acid), which hold the blueprint (genome) of who we are. The DNA is arranged in the form of two strands wrapped together to resemble a twisted ladder or 'double helix'. These amino acid strings are made up of nucleotides that are given the letter names of A, C, T and G (adenine, cytosine, thiamine and guanine), connected to bases or the rungs of the ladder. It is the order of the letters that determines the colour of our hair and eyes, our height, and our predisposition to certain diseases. In addition to nuclear DNA there is also genetic material found within the cytoplasm that surrounds the nucleus, mitochondrial DNA.

Defining idea... *'Genetics explains why you look like your father, and if you don't, why you should.'*
High school exam answer

As we have inherited our DNA from all our ancestors, however distant, they share with us a portion of this information. The closer the relationship, the more similar our DNA will be. It is therefore possible, in theory, to establish family links among individuals and families and even tribes and other indigenous groups.

One-namers are amongst the heaviest users of the DNA test, hoping to link families across the world. See IDEA 41, *The truly obsessed.*

Try another idea...

Of the 23 pairs of chromosomes, 22 are similar, the father supplying one set and the mother the other. The 23rd pair determines the sex: a female has the 23rd pair made up of two X chromosomes (Xcs), whereas a male has one X and one Y chromosome (Xcs and Ycs pair). Therefore, one of the 46 chromosomes in every male is a Ycs. This chromosome is passed almost unchanged from father to son, and any descendant strictly through the male line will have almost identical DNA on his Ycs as his ancestor. Therefore, distant cousins or those with the same surname can prove that they descend from the same male if they have the same Ycs DNA. It was this method that was used to show that President Thomas Jefferson had descendants through Sally Hemmings, one of his slaves.

Mitochondrial DNA (mtDNA) is transmitted from a mother to all her children, both male and female. But it is only passed on through the female line, and so stops with each son. Any individuals sharing mtDNA can therefore say that they descend from a common female ancestor strictly through the female line.

Claims that whereas family historians are only tracing their own family tree, the Human Genome Project is tracing that of humanity may seem far-fetched at the moment, but who can tell what the future will hold.

'Celibacy is not hereditary.'
First Law of Socio-genetics

Defining idea...

How did it go?

Q I had hoped that if I had a DNA test it might prove that I was descended from Horatio Nelson, which is the family tradition. Is that not the case, then?

A   *It depends on whether you are boy or girl and if you think the descent is through males or females. If you can get a known descendant of the admiral to have a DNA test then you may be able to prove you share an ancestor. Otherwise, you may need to pinch a bit of Nelson's hair from a museum and get that DNA tested! Just don't believe everything you see on CSI.*

Q What, then, can DNA testing be used for in tracing my past?

A   *DNA testing may help narrow research, a form of localisation, but it is still a long way from proving who your ancestors were. This is an area of research where there will certainly be significant strides forward in forthcoming years. So if you want to know if you are related to the Blenkinsops of Wagga Wagga, then a DNA test may help.*

37

Digitise your data

You don't have to be swamped by bits of paper. Get that scanner working overtime and let your computer take the strain.

Scanners are fun and very useful. Yes, there are some scanning techniques to learn, but once you've done it once or twice, then it becomes rather easy.

Over the past thirty years, many people have proclaimed the imminent arrival of the paperless office. This was predicted to revolutionise the way we work, learn and play – the work and education of the world would be converted into digital form, and lay the once popular paper medium to rest. However, along with the technology to facilitate the paperless office came the nemesis for those same predictions. This advance, known as the desktop printer, offered us the chance to use the theoretically obsolete paper to give us a permanent and easy-to-read copy of the information that we had purchased our computers specifically to store. Naturally, we obliged: we prefer not to have to read a large amount of text on a computer screen

Here's an
idea for
you...

Many believe that they should always scan at the greatest possible resolution. Not so. We need to choose a scan resolution based on the output device that will process that image, normally a video monitor or a printer; and, if the latter, the size of the print. The maths is complicated and incomprehensible to most, so experiment. Scan a good clean image at different resolutions – say at 72, 150, 300, 600 and 1200 dpi. Then print them out at A4 size on a good quality glossy paper and see the differences. Try smaller and larger print sizes. You will probably find 300 dpi is sufficient.

Defining
idea...

'Try to be conspicuously accurate in everything, pictures as well as text. Truth is not only stranger than fiction, it is more interesting.'
WILLIAM RANDOLPH HEARST (1863–1951) US newspaper publisher

unless we really have to; a piece of paper is much easier to read, and can be taken to places that a computer has never even seen.

A large number of human beings regard computers as unreliable, and would not trust them with so much as a scrap of information unless they really had to. Nevertheless, there are very many really sensible reasons for creating digitised copies of your documents, photographs, ephemera and the like. Security is only one of them, albeit an important one. The ability to share your information with others comes a close second, together with the fact that you can easily incorporate the images into your research notes, histories and anything else you care to create.

A flatbed scanner is very much like a photocopier, to the extent that it has a glass plate under a lid, and a moving light that scans across under it. Like a photocopier, a scanner allows you to scan photos, paper documents, books, magazines, large maps, or even three-dimensional objects such as coins and medals. However, instead of creating another piece of paper, it creates an image in memory – a digital image, with which we can do as we please.

In addition to the scanner itself, we must use software to operate it. Some scanner software can operate independently, and some cannot. Most image editor programs, such as Adobe Photoshop Elements or Corel's Paint Shop Pro, have a menu item allowing you to undertake and import a scan. The actual scanning process can be as easy or as complicated as you want. There is a learning curve to climb before you will be producing scans worthy of the originals, but the effort will certainly be worth it. Remember, read the instructions, ideally before all else fails.

Scanned images are ideal for including in a scrapbook project. See IDEA 40, *Creative Scrapbooking*.

Try another idea...

If you do scan into an image-editing program, or open a previously scanned image, then you can crop it, adjust its contrast and brightness and make other alterations. When the image is as you want it, then you can either print it or write it to a disk file, or both. Always save you image as a TIFF file. Both TIFFs and JPGs are industry standard formats but there are distinct advantages of selecting the TIFF option, not least quality. This will result in significantly larger file sizes but will be worth it in the long run.

Lastly, remember copyright. The rules are complicated but your local archive should be able to advise you, and there is a lot of information on the internet.

'Life is not significant details, illuminated by a flash, fixed forever. Photographs are.'
SUSAN SONTAG (1933–2005) US author, critic

Defining idea...

How did it go?

Q **How can I scan a document that is larger than the scanner bed?**

A *There are a few A3 (30 × 40 cm, 12 × 17 inch) flatbed scanners, but they are quite expensive. Otherwise, you can scan two or more partial images, and join them. The manual way is to open the images in a photo program, and enlarge the 'canvas size' of one image large enough to include the other part(s), and then copy them in. Use the layers option as it is then easier to align the various parts. Joining images this way is called stitching and some image editing programs include specific tools for stitching.*

Q **I get odd patterns in the images I scan. What's the reason for this?**

A *If you're scanning printed material (books, magazines, newspapers, postcards) instead of original photographs, then what you are getting are Moiré patterns, and this is to be expected. Magazine images are not at all the same thing as real photographs, as they are made up of thousands of tiny dots. When you undertake a scan you are imposing another matrix of dots and the two clash and produce a murky herringbone, crosshatched or dotted pattern. To improve your images, always undertake the original scan at at least 600 dpi and then use the 'descreen' option (present in most scanning software). With a little experimentation, much improved results are possible.*

38

Publishing on the web

**Keep it to yourself if you want, but you can share the
results of your sleuthing with the outside world using
the World Wide Web – and it's fun to do, too.**

The internet allows you to open the
window to your family's history from the
comfort of your own home.

Among the best of the online resources are the people out there, who you can
contact via newsgroups, mailing lists, etc. Through them you can tap into a vast
amount of information that you might not otherwise be aware of – the information
that is not systematically indexed or filed anywhere, or that is at too great a distance
to access directly.

If you have been researching your family history for a while and keeping a 'research
log' of what you have found where, the internet is an ideal medium for you to share
and circulate this information among others. The recent developments in new tools
have made it easier for people to publish online, reducing the technological hurdles
while increasing the breadth of options for publishing. So what are your options?

The term 'mailing list' was originally applied to a collection of names and addresses
used to send material to multiple recipients. The term now often includes the

Here's an idea for you...

Take the time to assess the information you have collected and decide on the best way to publish it for your purposes. Before you take any first steps, sample what's already on the internet to see how it works. For instance, you might decide that you want to set up your own website so other family members can see the fruits of your efforts as and when they wish.

people subscribed to such a list, so the group of subscribers are referred to as 'the mailing list', or simply 'the list'. An individual can subscribe or unsubscribe themselves to the list. Mailing lists tend to be quite specialist and those within family history are usually aimed at members of a society, those with interests in a specific area, occupation or specific surname.

A 'newsgroup' is the electronic equivalent of a message board, with the facility for messages to be posted from many users at different locations. They are mostly used for messages asking for help and advice, or writing about topics you feel may be of interest to others. Newsgroups are technically distinct from, but functionally similar to, 'discussion forums' on the World Wide Web. Internet forums have the additional facility for holding discussions. Web-based forums, which date from around 1995, perform a similar function as the dial-up 'bulletin boards' and internet newsgroups that were numerous in the 1980s and '90s. A sense of virtual community often develops around forums that have regular users. There are forums for a huge number of different family history topics.

An 'e-zine' is a regularly produced newsletter that is accessed electronically, either via a website or delivered as email. They were first developed during the 1980s. E-zines are typically tightly focused on a subject area such as an occupation or specific

Defining idea... **'Leave nothing for tomorrow which can be done today.'**
ABRAHAM LINCOLN (1809–1865)

surname. Some family and local history societies publish e-zines to provide information of interest to their members. An individual can subscribe or unsubscribe themselves to receive a copy. E-zines are ideal to distribute among family members to give updates on the family history.

To help you in the task of properly organising your information into a suitable format to get it online, look at IDEA 37, *Digitise your data.*

Try another idea…

'Blog' (short for weblog or web log) and is the term used to describe an 'online diary' or 'journal'. The blog format allows inexperienced computer users to make diary entries with ease. People blog poems, prose, complaints, daily experiences, family history and more, often allowing others to contribute. These have really come to the fore since 2001. A blog site typically contains a list of links, or blogroll, to other blogs that the blog author reads or affiliates with. As a diary of your family history studies, it's a fantastic way to share your experiences with others or simply to create a record for yourself. The distinction between blogs and forums can be somewhat blurred.

A website is just a collection of individual files stored on a web server (computer), usually with permanent access to the internet and usually accessed via a homepage with its own special address (URL). To date, it is estimated that there are over 80 million websites.

All of these are just alternative ways for you to circulate and access information regarding your family history. What does make them important is the input from the people that produce them.

'Curiosity is one of the most permanent and certain characteristics of a vigorous intellect.'
SAMUEL JOHNSON (1709–1784)
critic, poet and lexicographer

Defining idea…

How did it go?

Q How can I get people to create links to my website?

A *It is essential that the information on your website is relevant, concise, well organised and kept up to date so that people are going to want to link to it. Next look for other relevant local or family history websites that are going to attract the same type of person as you think would be interested in visiting your website. Lastly, contact those sites' webmasters enquiring if they would like to exchange links with you. Do bear in mind that many societies, archives and commercial sites do have set policies as to what type of sites they will link to.*

Q How can I tell which online publications contain trustworthy and reliable information and also make mine credible?

A *Whatever publishing medium is being used, any information is only as good as the person who presents it. The internet is no better or worse than any other method. However, the internet does magnify the problem because of the vast amount of material that can be found online and the ease with which it can be duplicated and links created. Additionally, people don't always quote the source of any information – thus, it is not always easy to validate the source or check for any additional information. You only really need to record enough information so that another researcher can determine what you have actually searched. Remember: without proof, there is no truth, so cite your sources and place more trust in others who do likewise.*

39

Grave responsibilities

Many Victorian cemeteries are places of outstanding historical interest, with fine examples of Victorian gothic funerary architecture. They offer great insights into past times.

Having departed this mortal coil their remains ended up somewhere: God's acre to Victorian cemeteries.

Burial grounds (as distinct from parish churchyards) were started by nonconformists in the seventeenth century; many more were established in the eighteenth century. These became known as 'cemeteries', taken from the Greek word *koimiteri*, meaning 'sleeping places'.

By the 1820s, there was a stark realisation that something had to be done about the overcrowding in London churchyards – disease was rife, with epidemics of cholera, typhus, typhoid and other unsavoury nasties. There were instances of body snatching, bodies left out to rot or not buried deep enough, and bodies cleared from graves too soon. This all came at a time of rapid growth – between 1801 and 1851, the population of Britain almost doubled, to over 27,000,000. New burial grounds had to be built and groups of financiers decided to purchase land outside the residential areas, on the outskirts of the metropolis in rural surroundings, and establish new cemeteries. The problem was not restricted to London and the other large cities. As people moved from the villages to the towns, many urban areas began to find there was an acute problem with space for burial. Up and down the land, the existing churchyards could not cope.

In 1827, the General Cemetery Company opened Kensal Green Garden Cemetery, rapidly followed by other cemetery companies opening further cemeteries in the following decades. These were established by private companies, with shareholders taking the profits. However, there was a general feeling that adequate burial facilities should be among the great public health improvements being made by local government, so during the 1840s several cities applied for Acts of Parliament to enable them to set up cemeteries with rate payers' money. From the 1850s, a series of Acts made the process cheaper and easier, and the great age of the municipal cemetery began.

The idea of landscaped public cemeteries came from Italy, France and Sweden. The winding, tomb-lined avenues and well-contrived vistas of the landscaped cemetery at Pere-Lachaise in Paris was widely admired. J. C. Loundon, *On the Laying Out, Planting, and Managing of Cemeteries* (1843) were widely influential and also led to improvements in the design of churchyards, with the construction of lych gates and new paths, and the planting of yews, cypresses and junipers alongside native species like lime and elm. Later, when Italian marble began to be imported into Britain, the ornate Victorian statuary began to appear. Such ideas also influenced the layout of public crematoria after the practice of cremation was legalised in 1884.

Here's an idea for you... **Find out if there are organised guided tours of your local Victorian burial ground. As an integral part of our Victorian heritage, they are extremely interesting places to visit and a knowledgeable guide will give you all sorts of pointers to the clues you should look for about Victorian funerary practices..**

Economic status could affect the location of burial. Brookwood Cemetery in Woking

(Surrey), opened as a private cemetery by the London Necropolis & National Mausoleum Company in 1854, and others competed to undertake contracts tendered each year by several London boroughs for the burial of their poor. Brookwood probably buried half of the dead from East London. To facilitate this, Waterloo Station had a special casket-loading platform, and trains containing funeral parties ran daily to a Gothic station built within the cemetery itself.

Over a century and a half after the opening of many of these cemeteries, a great number of the memorials, lovingly erected by friends and family, are no more. They became broken by time or vandalism and many were removed before any record of their inscriptions could be made. The typical Victorian cemetery demonstrates the attitudes of the time. Religion was all important, and many of these places were divided into Anglican and dissenters' sections.

Victorian monuments are a great source of information. Epitaphs 100 years ago were prolific and the highest standards of letter carving were reached. Victorians were keen to take their status into the next life through the grandeur of their monuments, and the words inscribed on them. But, more than that, the cemeteries are a lasting monument to social history, with the mourning etiquette, symbolism and social customs surrounding death and mourning an everlasting memorial to our Victorian ancestors.

> **Try another idea…**
>
> Once you have located the burial of your ancestor, why not see if you can discover an obituary in the local newspaper? Have a look at **IDEA 9, _All the news that's fit to print._**

> **Defining idea…**
>
> '**And, when he shall die, Take him and cut him out in little stars, And he will make the face of Heaven so fine, That all the world will be in love with night, And pay no worship to the garish sun.**'
> WILLIAM SHAKESPEARE

How did it go?

Q   Where do I find cemetery records?

A   *Cemetery records, particularly those prior to 1900, have often been deposited at local record offices, but some are still kept at the office on the site. The records usually give the name of the deceased, age, address and occupation, the date of death and of burial, and the position of the grave. You should also be able to discover who else is buried in the same plot. If you are really lucky, this may include several generations of your family. (One of my family graves lists seventeen members of the extended family.) These cemetery records are arranged chronologically, and are not usually indexed alphabetically. If the records are still on site there may be a search fee to locate a specific burial.*

Q   Among some family papers I have discovered a burial plot deed. Can you give me more information about this?

A   *Many families purchased a private plot for family burials. The family received a burial plot deed (proof of plot purchase) which needed to be shown at the cemetery when another burial was required in the plot. The deed should also include the plot number, allowing you to search in the cemetery grave book to discover who else is buried in he same plot. The cemetery may also hold plot records stating who originally purchased the plot and paid the burial fees. This may be a firm of undertakers who arranged the original burial.*

40

Creative scrapbooking

Have you ever thought of producing a book to pass down through the generations: a book of few words but many illustrations? It's well worth considering.

Get your artistic side into action and scrapbook the results of your research. Your imagination can run wild as you wield the glue gun and do crazy things with pinking shears.

If you have been wondering what you could leave behind for the generations to come, then perhaps a 'heritage scrapbook' might be the answer. But where do you begin?

There are two important questions to answer from the outset: first, what do you want to scrapbook, and second, who do you want to give the scrapbook to, if anyone? And, if you are thinking that scrapbooking involves those large, cheap and nasty books made from grey sugar paper that we used as kids, then think again. We are in another league here. All the rules about archival quality materials are obeyed. Scrapbooks – or to use the fancier term, 'heritage albums' – can combine photos,

The story you are trying to tell isn't limited to photos and family trees and cold, hard facts. Include other information in your album. Family traditions, a sketch plan of a house you once lived in, newspaper cuttings, pictures of tools of the person's trade, a map showing where the family originated, rubbings from gravestones. Experiment, make mistakes – it's fun. Enjoy.

annotations, drawings, newspaper clippings, mementos, and whatever your creative side can dream up.

So, what scrapbooking project might be suitable for a seeker of their past? Don't try to do a whole family tree – that would be daft. Choose a particular person or family group; or what you know about your house; or your local watering-hole; or the village; or your street; or a particular occupation; or a significant year; or … well, whatever you like. It might seem like a daunting task, but once you take that first step towards completing the first page of your first album, you'll be surprised at how easy it is.

Now you need to get organised. Once you have decided on your project – and start with something small if you haven't done this before – you need to gather together what you have and perhaps determine what you don't have so you can go scavenging. With all the elements at your fingertips, you'll get a clearer idea of what you are wanting to say with the pages you're about to create. Sketch out a 'storyboard', on the back of an envelope if you want, and then start arranging and rearranging the various bits. You should have already been thinking about captions and some narrative text because you won't get away with just pictures. Don't worry if your handwriting is less than perfect – there are lots of different computer fonts you can use, including some that look vaguely like handwriting.

'To forget one's ancestors is to be a brook without a source, a tree without a root.'

Chinese proverb

In addition to the items you are going to scrapbook, you will need to get hold of the pages to stick the bits and pieces to, and some 'embellishments', as they are called. You can buy starter kits, which include an album, a few

Understand those photos you are scrapbooking, so they are truly in context – see IDEA 46, *Families in focus.*

Try another idea…

pages and a selection of said embellishments. Look out for those aimed specifically at the heritage scrapbooker, but choose carefully because some of them are far from suitable. The great thing about scrapbooking is that you can throw out any of the rules about design you may read in any of the dozens of books on the subject, and just do your own thing. Mind you, you can get some really good ideas from these books, or from the hundreds of related websites.

Traditionally, scrapbook pages are 12 × 12 inches. Although there is nothing that necessarily restricts you to this format, bear in mind that if you go out to buy scrap-booking supplies, such as ready-made albums and pages, this is the only size you will find available in any quantities. Hence, you might as well accept it.

Another major decision to make is whether to use original items in your scrapbook, or copies of them. In some ways, if you scrapbook properly, then this can be as safe a place as anywhere to permanently house those valuable photographs, certificates and the like. But your sensibilities might be with mine, which means that you should only be using copies – good copies, mind you; indistinguishable from the originals. The originals can then be securely held elsewhere in the best archival conditions. Using copies also means that you can crop photographs and produce other images at more sensible sizes. And if you make a mistake you can throw the copy away and start again.

'Memories of our lives, of our works and our deeds will continue in others.'
ROSA PARKS (1913–2005) US black civil rights leader

Defining idea…

If you are reading this, you obviously believe your past is important. Be in no doubt – your family for generations to come will appreciate all the work that you put into creating your very own heritage scrapbooks.

How did it go?

Q **I keep hearing it suggested that scrapbooks should be kept simple. Doesn't that suggest a lack of creativity?**

A *Not at all. By keeping it simple it will concentrate the focus on the photographs, documents and ephemera. It also makes it easier to do. You shouldn't just look at other scrapbooks for ideas – snip ideas from any magazines or brochures that pass your way.*

Q **I'm a computer nerd. Can't I produce a virtual scrapbook so I can upload it to my website?**

A *Nothing nerdish in that ... well not much anyway. No, there is nothing to stop you producing scrapbook pages this way – many others already do, and it's a growing area. There are also lots of helpful scrapbook 'supplies' that can be bought as digital versions. Or you can produce your own, of course.*

41

The truly obsessed

For some, gathering every reference to a particular surname or place is their *raison d'être*. It may not be your idea of fun, but don't knock them because they could help you.

People who have unusual surnames have often been intrigued by them and are now using modern technology to build up lists of everybody sharing those names across the world.

Cabbin, Caberry, Cabin, Cackett, Cad, Cadd, Caddel, Caddell, Cadden, Caddle, Cade, Cadel, Cadell, Caden, Cadien, Cadle, Caide, Cailly, Cake, Caket, Calengham, Calenso, Calingham, Calinghelm, Calinhem, Callaff, Callangham, Callenso, Callingham, Calthorpe, Caltrup and Calverley are just some of the subjects of one-name studies. Our names are one of the things that differentiate us from anyone else. As you start to exhaust your personal research, and hit the proverbial 'brick wall', you might like to think about widening the scope of your search and collecting all instances of a particular name (and its variances), perhaps even worldwide, then organising them into family groups – a 'one-name study'. It provides the opportunity to continue with your interest in history, but with the hope that, one day, your elusive ancestors will be exposed. This does not, of course, have to be one of the surnames in your own lines – it could be that of a distant ancestor's husband or wife, or just a familiar name that grabs your imagination.

The gathering and in-depth study of a particular name can give you a fantastic insight into its distribution. Tracking back via genealogical methods will also show you all of the name's earliest variants. In addition, such research allows you to make good use of some of more unusual datasets and indexes, such as Hearth Tax, Land Tax or Window Tax.

There is a need for real commitment to undertake this type of study because it has a much wider scope and opens wide the ability to communicate with other researchers. If you choose to research a bloodline, you will eventually come into contact with cousins. They may be several generations removed but they are still cousins. It is challenging to be a specialist on your 'name' and very rewarding to be able to help people to extend their own family trees. However, be warned: it is very absorbing and you will inevitably get side-tracked, fascinated by the history and events that surrounded and influenced these other families, perhaps even explaining why they immigrated, migrated or emigrated.

Here's an idea for you...
To discover more about your earlier ancestors, try delving into the extraordinary records of the manorial courts, which can reveal the history of communities from the twelfth century. A listing of the surviving records exists in the Manorial Documents Register at The National Archives.

A one-name study can also concentrate on particular aspects, such as geographical distribution of a name and the changes in that distribution over the centuries, or attempt to reconstruct the genealogy of as many lines as possible bearing that name. A common ambition is to try to identify the origins of the name, especially if it appears to derive from a place name, but for many names there will not be a single origin.

Some researchers choose to transcribe and index original sources. Others use existing transcripts and contemporary lists, like trade directories, to collect information about the inhabitants of one place or one name. The clever researcher, however, will use any sources that are available to them. Some choose just to determine which records and indexes exist about their area – be they found in a book, on microfiche, CD, or on the internet – to help other researchers.

When dealing with larger amounts of information, proper data management is essential in order to allow good storage and retrieval. There's more on this in IDEA 19, *Files, formats and family trees*, and IDEA 37, *Digitise your data*.

Try another idea…

People collect information on all sorts of things, creating databases of just about every class of record that might be of use to the family or local historian – everything from apprenticeship records to tithe lists, from tax rolls to debtors' lists, and from indexes of foundlings to lists of vagrants. Many of these smaller specialist indexes have not been widely published but may be held by individuals or societies.

One-place studies can also be a very interesting avenue of research – collecting all information about the area where you live, came from, or from whence your ancestors hailed. They are also a useful source for the rest of us for gaining more information about the places from which our ancestors originated. Organising a one-place study can lead you to very specific and unusual sources for local and family history, by virtue of the fact that you are researching all the surnames within a given area. The amount of information you collate really depends on how far you want to go – your options are never ending …

'A fanatic is one who can't change his mind and won't change the subject.'
WINSTON CHURCHILL (1874–1965)

Defining idea…

Q **How do I go about starting a one-name study?**

A *You may find it useful to start by assessing how rare or common the name you are interested in is. You can look at its geographical distribution to determine just how big a task you are taking on. Some people choose to be selective and research names that are relatively rare; others are working on larger studies with world populations of tens of thousands. You can then start collecting information on a systematic basis. Many of the initial sources you will use are the same as those used by other genealogists before spreading your wings in other directions to the more unusual sources. If someone is already doing a one-name study of your desired name, or even a one-place study, why not approach them and offer to join forces? It could be of massive benefit to us all.*

Q **Where will I find it most easy to locate information from one-name/one-place studies?**

A *Much of this information is now available not only on microfilm or microfiche but also on CD-ROM or the internet. People often register their one-name or place-name study with the appropriate organising body. There are also specialist publications outlining what indexes are being compiled and where you can find them.*

42

The Lloyd George Domesday

Often referred to as the 'Second Domesday Survey', this is one of the most easily accessible and helpful sources for twentieth-century research.

In 1910, the government decided to survey every property in England and Wales. Owners, occupiers, values and descriptions of the properties are all recorded, with even the occasional rough plan thrown in.

Following the introduction of old-age pensions in 1908 and other social reforms, Lloyd George also faced the need to fund the building of new 'dreadnought' battleships. Hence, he needed to raise taxes, and the method he chose was to revert to a land tax based on a comprehensive national survey.

The Finance (1909–1910) Act – with the introduction of a tax of 20% on the increased value of property between 30 April 1909 and when it was sold – provoked a political crisis that led to the loss of power by the House of Lords. In the long term, however, historians are eternally grateful to Lloyd George for the survey, which revealed the extent of property ownership throughout the country. Very

If you know the rough location of an ancestor's family, then by looking at the records created under the 'Lloyd George Domesday' survey, you should be able to locate the family just before the First World War and discover where they were living, if they were land owners or tenants, how much rent they paid and possibly obtain an account of the property. Some records will be at your local county record office but a trip to The National Archives (for England and Wales), or to the National Archives of Scotland, or to the Public Record Office of Northern Ireland, will prove extremely worth while.

Defining idea…

'**Well! Some people talk of morality, and some of religion, but give me a snug little property.**'
MARIA EDGEWORTH (1767–1849)
The Absentee

simply, it shows the owner and occupier of every piece of land in the country at the time of the survey, and often includes a good description of the property itself. The survey was not completed until the autumn of 1915.

There are three sets of records resulting from the survey: the Field Books, the Valuation Office Plans and the Valuation Books.

Each unit of property was assigned an assessment number (sometimes also called a hereditament number) and plans based on the Ordnance Survey sheet maps were drawn up as the chief means of reference to the other records created in the course of valuation. Two sets of plans were created: the working plans used in the course of the original valuation and the record plans made after that valuation was completed. Those working plans that survive are in the custody of local record offices, and the record plans are now held at The National Archives (TNA).

As a first step towards the systematic valuation required by the 1910 Act, copies of the Income Tax Schedule A Registers kept by inspectors of taxes were made available to district valuers (Income Tax Schedule A being payable on income from the ownership of lands, tenements, hereditaments or heritages in the United Kingdom). These copies were produced in the form of bound volumes (the so-called Domesday Books). Those Valuation Books that survive are in local record offices, with the exception of a number for the City of London and City of Westminster, which are held at TNA.

If the family were farmers, or even evacuated to a farm during the Second World War, then IDEA 43, *The National Farm Survey*, will be of interest.

Try another idea…

The final record, compiled after the survey was completed, was written up in small bound volumes called Field Books. These are now in The National Archives. The amount of information entered in the Field Books varies considerably, but usually includes the names of owner and occupier, the owner's interest (freehold, copyhold, etc.), details of tenancy (term and rent), and the area covered by the property. Other details recorded may include the date of erection, number of rooms, state of repair, liability for rates, insurance and repairs, date(s) of previous sale(s) and, sometimes, a sketch plan of the property. Figures entered for the purpose of valuation normally include the market value simply of the whole property and the market value of the site divested of structures, timber and plants.

If you are trying to track down the owners or occupiers of a particular house, farm, smallholding or other property, or just wanting to know a little more about the place where an ancestor's family lived, then the records resulting from this survey can be extremely helpful.

'Be it ever so humbug, there's no place like home.'
NOEL COWARD (1899–1973) English actor, composer and playwright

Defining idea…

How did
it go?

Q **It is great to read a description of the property my great-grand-parents and their children lived in. Some other properties have a little sketch plan but there isn't one for mine. Why?**

A *Plans were usually drawn for farms and other buildings, but less frequently for smaller properties and houses. If the building was one of several in a street that were identical, then possibly the surveyor only drew the first one, so try looking elsewhere in the Field Book. I have even come across a contemporary postcard stuck in a Field Book as a general illustration of the area.*

Q **Is there anywhere else I can find information about a particular property I have discovered in these records?**

A *This is where a local studies library may be able to help considerably. There you may find photographs of the area or other illustrations. Don't forget to look for postcards as well. If it is in London or another large urban area, they may have much larger scale plans, or insurance plans. And if the area had only recently been developed, then there may be deeds or other documents that will add to your knowledge.*

The National Farm Survey

During the Second World War, every farm or similar holding of five acres or more was surveyed. Owners, occupiers and the state of cultivation are all detailed. Those details are there for you now.

When the Second World War began in September 1939, Britain was faced with the urgent need to increase the production of food. Every productive area was assessed.

As soon as war broke out, food imports were drastically cut. A ploughing-up campaign soon commenced and large expanses of land (some that had not seen the plough since medieval or even prehistoric times) were prepared for cultivation.

In June 1940, a farm survey was initiated with the purpose of further increasing food production. Farms were graded in terms of their productive state: A, B or C. These categories related more to the physical condition of the land than to the managerial efficiency (or otherwise) of the farmer. Nevertheless, it was also vital to assess the ability of each farmer to play his part in the national food production plan. In cases of gross inefficiency or dereliction, land was placed under government control and labour organised accordingly. Between June 1940 and the early months of 1941 some 85% of the agricultural area was surveyed – all but the smallest farms.

Once the short-term objective of increasing food production had been met, thought was given to implementing a more general National Farm Survey with a longer-term purpose of providing data that would form the basis of post-war planning. Contemporary press releases issued by the Ministry of Agriculture and Fisheries included historical notes on the original Domesday Survey and on other land surveys that had been carried out over the centuries.

Every farm and holding of five acres and more was to be surveyed, including those of market gardeners, horticulturists, and poultry-keepers. Holdings of one to five acres, representing less than 1% of the total area of crops and grass, were subject to a separate survey. The National Farm Survey was begun in the Spring of 1941 and largely completed by the end of 1943. It was undertaken largely by experienced, practical farmers who visited and inspected each farm and interviewed the farmer.

Both the individual farm records of the National Farm Survey, 1941–1943, and the maps, which serve as a graphic index to the farms, are held at The National Archives (TNA). The individual farm record is made up of four forms. Three, dated 4 June 1941,

tere's an idea for you...

There is every likelihood that where you now live was once farmland – and, if not you, then perhaps where your parents or grandparents lived. Have a look at the National Farm Survey as it is a great place to start to see what was there during and around the Second World War. The surviving records can also be the stepping stones to earlier surveys, such as the 'Lloyd George Domesday', the mid-nineteenth century tithe commutations, and earlier estate surveys. So, while you are in the library or record office see what else they have for those parcels of land that were part of your past.

were completed by the farmer himself: one showing details of small fruit, vegetables, and stocks of hay and straw; the second, agricultural land; and the third showing labour, motive power, rent, and length of occupancy. The fourth form was the Farm Survey, the 'primary survey' that was obtained in the field by inspection and interview.

Farmland was what comprised most of the country's manors. Find out more about land ownership going back centuries from IDEA 32, *Manors maketh man*.

Try another idea…

One of the most controversial parts of the Survey, and the one for which the Survey is often remembered, lies under section D of the Primary Farm Survey, 'Management'. It was here that the recorder had to classify the farm as A, B, or C (performing well, fairly, or badly), and if B or C and due to 'personal failings', he was also obliged to supply additional details. Of the 300,000 farms and holdings classified by the Survey, 58% were A, 37% B, and 5% C.

In addition to the forms, maps of the farms were produced showing their boundaries and the fields contained in them. At best, which is rare, each farm is identified by different colour washes – sometimes a full wash over the whole area of the farm but often just the boundaries highlighted.

As a source for local and family historians, the records of the National Farm Survey are of great value. For the historical geographer, these records present an enormous database of land ownership and land usage in mid-twentieth century Britain.

'A farm is an irregular patch of nettles bounded by short-term notes, containing a fool and his wife who didn't know enough to stay in the city.'
S. J. PERELMAN (1904–1979)
American humorist and screenwriter

Defining idea…

How did it go?

Q **My gran was evacuated to a farm from London during the Second World War. Is this National Farm Survey a good place to find more about where she went and what sort of place it was?**

A *The Survey is, by its nature, very matter-of-fact and so you will be able to discover how the farm ticked over and a little about the farmer too. Children's memories are often distorted, being largely based on whether they were happy or sad at the time, so, if your gran is still around, she should be able to give you some reminiscences and you will be able to draw your own conclusions as to whether she had a good time or not.*

Q **Is there nothing I can see locally – do I have to visit The National Archives?**

A *Sorry, but to use the National Farm Survey records, a trip to Kew is necessary. However, records such as these should never be used in isolation and it is probable that your local record office will have other information on the farms that interest you – and perhaps something about the owners or the occupiers of the farms as well.*

44

Bricks and mortar

The architectural heritage of the British Isles is one of the richest in the world. Even your own home will have a story to tell about the history of your area.

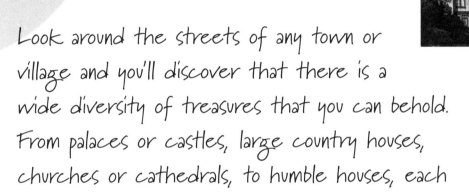

Look around the streets of any town or village and you'll discover that there is a wide diversity of treasures that you can behold. From palaces or castles, large country houses, churches or cathedrals, to humble houses, each has its special place in our past.

An examination of the architectural evidence and the style in which a house was built and the materials used can indicate an approximate age for the construction. It is important to remember that since time began people have been improving and extending their properties, so building may have been undertaken over a considerable number of years.

One of the first things to look at is where the house is built. Development tended to start near the centre of a community. The original plot may have subsequently been

Here's an idea for you… **To discover what your home looked like prior to you taking up residence, check for any photographs. Ask previous occupiers, neighbours, local or family history societies. Also check for any events – such as a street party for the Queen's Silver Jubilee, VE Day, summer barbeque etc. – during which your street or house might have been photographed.**

subdivided, so a plot of land that originally had just one dwelling on it may now have two or three.

Look at the type, style and size of the bricks used. These were often stamped with the name of the maker, which again may hold clues because you can pinpoint when they were in production. However, in older properties when extending or renovating it is now common practice to use recycled bricks to try to match the originals, so beware. If you have a cellar, pay it special attention because this is likely to define the original construction.

Examine the roof space. Can you see single brick spaces in the walls? These would have been used as 'keys' for wooden scaffolding long before the advent of modern metal pole scaffolding. Look at the style of the beams and structure within the loft space – the styles changed over the years as different building methods developed. Look at what the actual roofing material is, but bear in mind that the roof may have been replaced at some time. Also look at the roofs on nearby buildings. What were the local building materials? Was it thatching, local tiles or slates?

Look at the chimney stacks and how they relate to the fireplaces within the property. Are they original or were they added at a later date? If they have been removed is there evidence of what previously existed?

If your property is a timber-framed house, see how much timber has been used in the exterior and is showing. The closer the beams, the more money spent on wood, giving an indication of the social standing of the original owners.

What do you do when there are no photographs available for the house or other particular building that interests you? How do you discover what it was like? See Idea 45, *Plots and plans*.

Try another idea…

Design and tastes change over time, and this will be reflected in the internal structure of your home. The windows and door frames can give tell-tale clues about the evolution of your house. The shape/type of windows and the keystones above them can all give an indication of age. If you do not have original windows and door frames, try to look at the other properties on your street for clues.

The staircase can be one of the oldest features in a house, and in older or higher status buildings one of the central structures. Look for any carvings or decorations, along with any exposed wood or panelling, all of which can indicate the age of a property.

It is unlikely that any original decoration survives. However, remnants of past decoration may be found hidden away in the corners of cupboards. Diaries and insurance records, particularly fire insurance claims, contain listings and descriptions of houses and their contents. Probate inventories may list the deceased's belongings on a room-by-room basis. A number of publications are available should you want to discover more about the internal aspects of a property and original decoration styles.

'We shape our buildings; thereafter they shape us.'
WINSTON CHURCHILL (1874–1965)

Defining idea…

How did it go?

Q   We live in a fairly new house – built in the 1990s – so it doesn't have a lot of history. Is there anything of potential interest we could look into?

A   *You could take a look at what was there before your home was built. Particularly if you live in an urban area, there may have been houses or factories or workshops on that site previously. Ask your older neighbours what they know or remember about the area – you may be surprised exactly what people do know. Check out earlier photographs of the area. Sources for these include local history societies, newspapers and commercially produced books and, of course, the internet.*

Q   When trying to determine the true age of a property, what are the pitfalls?

A   *A building can often be constructed on the site of an earlier building. This may be the result of the loss of the older building through neglect, to optimise commercial potential or to improve on the standard of housing in an area. Many rebuilt structures incorporate material from an earlier building that might suggest that the main structure is older than it really is. When Coventry's city walls were demolished, for example, the stone was recycled into other buildings. Often building styles continued in an area even though the national trend was different. Conversely, many modern buildings are constructed in an older style (sometimes with reclaimed materials), which can make a property appear older than it really is. It is important to cross-reference documentary and architectural evidence to minimise these risks.*

45

Plots and plans

In the absence of photographs, there are many other records that will give you a strong flavour of what your house, or other particular building of interest, was like in the past.

One of the main attractions of house history is that it combines many disciplines, requiring you to unearth clues about the lives of former inhabitants and discover more about the local community.

A good way to begin your quest is by asking your neighbours what they know about your house or street. Also look for printed histories of the area. Try to locate any surviving title deeds and conveyance documents relating to the house. If you don't have a mortgage, then you may already have them; otherwise, check if your solicitor or mortgage company hold them or if they are deposited in the local archives. These will give a description of the house, its position, plot dimensions, names of previous owners and occupiers and details of transactions and mortgages and the date of construction.

Here's an idea for you... **Many local record offices produce information leaflets detailing how to trace the history of a house located in their area using their record holdings. Make sure you check this out before starting your research because it can save you a great deal of time and effort.**

The system of compulsory land registration now operating in England and Wales developed gradually during the nineteenth and twentieth centuries. The land register can be consulted by members of the public regarding current ownership. Full information can be found on the Land Registry's website. You should also attempt to 'place' your house in the locality by determining what parish and borough it was in – this will open other avenues for research.

You can also determine approximately when your house was built by seeing when it first appears on the large scale Ordnance Survey maps (from the early 1800s). By consulting consecutive editions it is possible to track the development of an individual building, including any alterations and changes in use and plot size. In addition, there are tithe and enclosure maps covering the early part of the nineteenth century, Valuation Office records and maps (the Lloyd George Domesday, 1910) and National Farm Survey records and maps (1940–1943). These are invaluable when consulting street directories and are best used in tandem with them. A Return of Landowners was published in 1873 and lists landowners on a county-by-county basis.

From the 1850s, local councils took advantage of new powers to require developers to submit plans for approval prior to the commencement of building. The resulting building plans allow you to see what the original or intended layout of the house was, plus you can also follow any subsequent changes to a property over the years. Often the plans also show the various elevations of a property – enabling you to see what the building looked like even in the absence of photographs.

Recent estate agent details may still be with the agent. Sale catalogues and prospectuses can give details about properties and former owners. Where they survive, they will be found among deposited company or solicitors' papers.

Rate books also give the names of owners and householders, and the values of their properties. Although a small number date back to the sixteenth century, survival is particularly good from the late eighteenth century onwards, properties being listed on a street-by-street basis.

For more information about how to examine the more permanent features of your home and start your own home survey, look through IDEA 44, *Bricks and mortar*.

Try another idea...

Many other taxes were based on property, and you can use surviving returns (which can be found mainly at The National Archives) to trace property through the tax liability of their occupants. These include Hearth Tax 1662–1688, Land Tax from 1692 and Window Tax from 1696.

If you wish to find out more about individuals, this can be done via information from birth, death and marriage certificates, parish registers, census listings, wills, death duty records, electoral registers and poll books, telephone directories, newspapers, journals and magazines.

Investigating the history of your house is an exciting and informative discipline, bringing you into direct contact with the past. Most of the records involved are easily accessible and can be found in your local archives. Your research can become as detailed as you want, combining local history and genealogy. And more importantly it's really good fun!

'A doctor can bury his mistakes but an architect can only advise his clients to plant vines.'
FRANK LLOYD WRIGHT
(1867–1959) architect

Defining idea...

How did
it go? **Q** **I haven't got time to do the history of my home at present but what can I do to preserve the information and memories that I have?**

A *It is important to try to preserve all types of history. One of the things that you could do is to share the older pictures of your home with the local historical society or local studies library if they don't already have copies. If you can, date the pictures and give a brief description and background to them. The many local history groups throughout the British Isles can offer you an enormous amount of help and advice and they publish a variety of books and journals relating to the communities they cover.*

Q **I know that my house is several hundred years old but I am struggling to find it in the earlier records. Why is that?**

A *Remember that names or numbers of houses are not always given, particularly in the earlier records. With increased development, the street may have been renumbered or even renamed. Thus, 1 Cromwell Street may now be 25 Mandela Road. Although all the houses in a road may look alike from the outside, they may have been built over a period of perhaps 20 years, and not in order, resulting in some numbers being 'missed out'. Registers recording these alterations may occasionally be found with the records of the local authority. The actual boundaries of a town will also have changed with time.*

46

Families in focus

Discovering old family photographs is enormously satisfying, but what do you actually see? Open your mind to *all* of what they are really telling you.

Diane Arbus, the American photographer, wrote: 'A photograph is a secret about a secret. The more it tells you the less you know.' She was more than right, too.

Anyone researching their past will start by scouring their own homes, and those of relatives, for any family memorabilia. For most, of all the family documents we hope to uncover, none are more exciting in their discovery than photographs of ancestors whose likenesses before that moment were quite unknown.

Before the introduction of wide-scale photography in the 1850s, the production of visual images was in the hands of painters and draughtsmen. Their skills necessarily included the ability to flatter and deceive. However, the idea that the camera cannot lie is far from true. Kafka called the camera a 'mechanical mistake-thyself'. As with all aspects of research you must be prepared to question the evidence.

Here's an idea for you... **Look again at your collection of old, and perhaps not so old, photographs. It is difficult, but try to put aside the passion they frequently instil. Ask a friend what they think they see before you explain who the people are and what they mean to you. The great-uncle you hated all your life, because he refused to take you fishing when you were five, may in fact have been quite a nice old buffer, and someone else may see that in him.**

Defining idea... *'Photographers deal in things which are continually vanishing and when they have vanished there is no contrivance on earth which can make them come back again.'*
HENRI CARTIER-BRESSON
(1908–2004) photographer

Firstly you need to remember that the photograph performed a quite different function than it does today. We have moved from the time when the sole purpose was to record a likeness or event for posterity – as the paintings that came before did – to a time when we click away like there is no tomorrow. Photography now, as Susan Sontag puts it, is as commonplace as 'sex and dancing'. In the early days, photographers were all professionals or very skilled amateurs. They were very much in control and frequently wanted to communicate some particular thought or emotion with their work.

Albert Einstein knew a thing or two, about relatives as well as relativity: 'A photograph never grows old. You and I change, people change all through the months and years, but a photograph always remains the same. How nice to look at a photograph of mother or father taken many years ago. You see them as you remember them. But as people live on, they change completely. That is why I think a photograph can be kind.' Unfortunately, what

Einstein left out of the equation – he knew something about equations too – is that as we change so do our memories, warped by time and experience. Too often we see what we want to see. Family photographs don't change, but the stories we tell about them just might. Two people looking at the same photograph rarely see the same thing, particularly if they both knew the person concerned and had different experiences of them.

Photos have a unique value: look after them. To develop your collection, see IDEA 49, Cameras are not just for holidays!

Try another idea...

It is not only portrait-style family photographs that we need to be careful about. Many images of people at work or going about their daily business were carefully posed to put them in their very best light and to create an artistic composition. The images in collections held in local archives across the country also need to be very carefully scrutinised. Always ask yourself the question, why? Why was that particular photograph taken; why that view at that time?

Also be wary of rogue photos in your collection: not family or friends at all. Just as now, in Victorian time tens of thousands of celebrity photographs were sold, including royalty, actors and performers, and others on the then A list. If you cannot identify that little old lady, it might just be Florence Nightingale.

Undeniably, photographs are the most exciting of all the documents we collect. Some of us are luckier than others in the numbers we have, but we all cherish the memories they keep alive. Whether they really give an insight into an ancestor who we never actually knew is debatable.

'It takes a lot of imagination to be a good photographer. You need less imagination to be a painter because you can invent things.'
DAVID BAILEY (1938–) photographer

Defining idea...

Q **I've got several old photos but I have no idea who they are. They are quite small, the size of a credit card, and stuck on card. Does this format come from a particular era?**

A *What you have are probably* cartes de visite, *which were introduced into England in 1860. The clues you need to look for include: the name and address of the photographer (usually on the back) – trade directories will tell you when he was in business there; the backdrop – these changed with time; fashion details – the actual clothes can be misleading as these could be worn for many years, because of hand-me-downs, so look at hair-styles and accessories which were easily changed. There are lots of books that will help you with these last two ideas.*

Q **Why does everyone look so miserable in old photographs?**

A *There is a belief that this was because of the long exposures needed and the various contraptions that were used to stop people moving. The truth is quite different. Simply, you were not expected to smile when you had your picture taken – it was not what you did and to do so was unacceptable and would spoil the photograph.*

47

Places in perspective

Many elements of the landscape are invisible. Recognise the clues, though, and you'll discover your surroundings far beyond your normal pedestrian point of view.

Whether you live in a rural village, a Midland town or a London suburb, its history will have followed the pattern of open field to enclosed land to village to town to city.

Wherever you now live, this pattern of change is often still visible and will almost certainly have been recorded in some way. Man's creation of the present day urban and rural landscape has been a long process: as far back as the Neolithic period, people were busy clearing land for cultivation and grazing, and for establishing settlements. It is from the Roman period, and particularly since the Norman Conquest, that these changes become more apparent.

Documentary sources will provide the greatest amount of material for study and any investigations should start at the local studies library to see what relevant material has already been published. Documents are not the only source, though: there is an enormous amount of information stored in the buildings and the land itself,

Here's an idea for you… **Once you have identified a lost feature from the landscape on a map or in a published local history – whether it is a deserted village from the fourteenth century, a significant building or estate now broken up, or the pub that used to be at the end of the road – your search has only just begun. You then need to discover if any evidence remains on the ground. So, with map and camera, set off to see what you can find. Leave the spade at home – that's for the real experts. Some features may be obvious, others less so. Probably the boundary will still be recognisable, its 'extent' now defining something else: separating the housing estate from the superstore. Perhaps there may be the remains of a wall or garden. The features you noticed from an aerial photograph may be invisible at ground level, but that in itself is a discovery.**

which can give up its secrets to the inquisitive mind and an educated eye.

At the local studies library, start by actually asking for help. The knowledge held in the heads of most local archivists is quite incredible: certainly they usually know their collections inside out and will probably be able to point you to the right sources without the necessity of your searching card or computer catalogues. Initially look for any visual evidence of the changing face of the street, village, parish or town – old postcards, drawings, photographs, watercolours. Does the *Victoria History of the Counties of England*, the *Survey of London* or similar work include what you want? Has *Country Life* published an article covering a local country house?

Maps and plans are undoubtedly the sources of most use at this stage and will tell you more. The purpose is to identify what now remains of those ancient boundaries, or field names or those of owners or occupiers in the names of the roads and estates around us now.

Anyone who has seen the TV series *Time Team* will know how aerial photography is used to identify features in the landscape that cannot be seen from the ground. When the sun is low in the sky and shadows are more marked, features such as deserted villages and Roman villas can be identified. Crop marks are also used, variations in the colour and intensity occurring where the earth was disturbed, even many centuries ago.

England is full of abandoned villages. Some were deserted in medieval times, possibly as a result of the 'great plague' of 1348–49, while others were taken over by the armed forces, such as Imber on Salisbury Plain. Industrial decline emptied even more. The eighteenth and nineteenth century enclosures of common land, incorporating small plots into bigger, more efficient farms drove countless thousands from the land. Examples come from very recent years: the land once occupied by the terraced houses and tinplate works in two hamlets in Llanelli is now an 18-hole championship golf course.

I had a colleague once who said perspective was when you thought things disappeared but really they didn't. In a strange way, perhaps he was right.

To find out more about how to get the most from maps and plans, go through IDEA 17, *How does the land lie?*

Try another idea…

'That series of inventions by which man from age to age has remade his environment is a different kind of evolution – not biological, but cultural evolution …'
JACOB BRONOWSKI (1908-1974)
English historian, mathematician

Defining idea…

How did it go?

Q **I'm quite interested in the industries that were in the area where I now live. What sort of evidence might I find about them?**

A *There is a great deal that remains from early industries that deserves recording and preserving. At one end you have the artefacts that were produced: the pots, the drainage pipes, the cast-iron grates, the pillar-boxes and so forth. At the other end you have the factories, the mines and the workshops and the machinery that produced the goods. The sources for researching industrial archaeology are the same: published research, maps and plans, the archives of the companies themselves, which may survive in the local record office.*

Q **My cousin every so often goes and helps 'beat the bounds'. What is she up to, then?**

A *Before detailed maps were available, the only way parish boundaries were remembered was by word of mouth and by the beating-of-the-bounds, an ancient custom carried out in Rogation Week. The parish priest, the constable and a throng of inhabitants would make a perambulation of the parish boundary so that its course would remain in their collective memory. Now, many villages still carry on the tradition, including the eating and drinking that was always associated with the event.*

48

A rue with a view

See your street and community through the eyes of those residents of earlier times by discovering contemporary postcards of the area. They provide a fascinating snapshot of the past.

It is difficult to adequately describe or illustrate the streets on which our ancestors walked or the churches where they were baptised, married or buried. Postcards can paint those pictures.

Postcards had their origins in 'message cards', which were introduced in the 1820s and were posted with an envelope. The modern postcard developed on the Continent following an earlier idea originating in the United States in early 1861. The first true postcards, or 'correspondence cards', were issued on 1 October 1870 by the British Post Office and bore the new British name 'Post Card'. Pictures were yet to come, but many of the earlier cards carried advertisements. The first picture postcards were available in the early 1890s and were thought to be of Scarborough.

Subject cards were published initially, featuring things like the Boer War and royal events. In 1902, for the first time the Post Office allowed both address and message to be written on one side of the card, leaving the whole of the other side for a picture. Britain thus became the first country to introduce the 'divided back' postcard format that we know today. Around this time, the sizes of cards were also standardised. Postcards rapidly became the medium for transmitting short messages to friends and family and were used very much as we use email, texting and telephones today. They were cheap and reliable; with up to seven postal deliveries a day, a card could be written and delivered on the same day. People started to buy them to keep as souvenirs as well as to send to family and friends.

A magazine was published between 1900 and 1907 to cater for the interest, with national publishers meeting the demand by issuing postcards on every subject imaginable while local photographers recorded and published interesting local events. Millions of postcards went through the postal system every week, with a high proportion finishing up in someone's album, only to be rediscovered many years later.

Here's an idea for you... **Try collecting postcards of the same view of an area, taken over a number of years. This will allow you to compare and contrast the scenes and see just how the area has changed.**

The First World War changed the emphasis of the subjects featured, and with the introduction of the telephone the use of picture postcards began to decline, never to really regain the same sort of use or popularity. Fewer types of cards were published as most firms involved in postcard production either changed direction or simply stopped trading, postcards being relegated to something just sent to friends and family when you went on holiday.

Postcards began to regain popularity as an advertising and art medium in the 1970s, and today they can be found in high street shops, cafés and entertainment venues. Since the 1950s, old postcards have become collectable items, a 'must have' for a growing number of people.

For another 'view' of the landscape, looking at those aspects that are invisible within a straightforward photograph, see IDEA 47, Places in perspective.

Try another idea…

So where are the best places to locate postcards? The Post Card Traders Association organises regular specialist postcard fairs around the country. Postcards can also be found at local history, family history, book and stamp fairs, antique and second-hand shops, car boot sales and from the various online auction sites. Another valuable source, of course, are family members – you never know what asking them might reveal.

There are many local and specialist postcard clubs, covering such things as aviation, canals, Concorde, Festival of Britain, football, national piers, and railways. There is also a Postcard Index, a collection of thousands of postcards dating from the 1890s up to 1950 indexed by the recipient's name, address and date that may help you locate postcards relevant to your family.

Nothing can compare with the information that you can obtain from a postcard and the way it can cater for all interests. Whether you're interested in a particular subject or interested in the events and fashions or social history of the past century, the postcard encapsulates it all.

'Life is a great big canvas, and you should throw all the paint on it you can.'
DANNY KAYE (1913–1987) stage, film and television entertainer

Defining idea…

How did
it go? **Q   How much can I expect to pay for a postcard?**

A   *Even quite old cards can cost under £1, though the best street scenes can
cost much more. Pictures of churches are very good value for money. For
special subject cards (such as the Titanic, suffragettes and football teams),
you can pay over £100, while ordinary themes (flowers and country views)
can be quite cheap. Generally, the card's age doesn't provide an indication
of cost: a card from the 1970s may sell for more than one from the Edward-
ian era, for instance. As with stamp collecting, you should only start collecting postcards for illustrating your family or local history or because you
like the subject matter, and not for possible financial gain – it is very easy
to lose money by attempting to collect for profit.*

**Q   I've been given an album containing old picture postcards. How
can I discover more about them?**

A   *If the postcards are not too tightly glued into the album see if you can
carefully remove them without damaging any. Have a really close look at
the picture itself, to determine any special relevance to your family (e.g.
is it a picture of people or places that you recognise?). Looking at the rear
side, the stamp, postmark, message and address can all tell you something
about the sender and the recipient. Do you recognise the address to which
it was posted, does the message make reference to your family or their
friends or home town?*

49

Cameras are not just for holidays!

Or how to make sure you create your own modern-day photo archive.

Perhaps it's time to re-evaluate and even return to some of the reasons why our ancestors created the photographs they did.

In the days before television, Happy Snaps and the mass media, family photographs and the recording of place and time had a significance and meaning which we have possibly lost, to our own and our descendants' detriment. Every day, millions of images are forced at us from books, magazines and newspapers, through advertising, pornography and the internet, and in brochures and on packaging. On the whole, our own efforts pale into insignificance compared with all that is around us. And this, in spite of the fact that we take more and more and more pictures of our own every year.

Perhaps it is all too easy now. With the digital revolution, taking pictures is cheap: effectively free once you have the camera, or the mobile camera-phone. There's no

Here's an idea for you... **Choose a photograph from your family album or take your own photograph or series of photographs: a person or group, your town, your house, people at work. Now, why did you take, chose, or identify that particular image? What is it that might be of interest to future generations, not necessarily your own family's? An archive is for the future but of the present. Do your choices match those needs?**

need for film, no need for processing, and the results are more or less instantaneous. The considered portrait or the carefully judged streetscape are mostly from the past or from today's professionals, and even they are now more interested in artistic merit than a record of reality. Snaps are great: they capture the moment and in many ways benefit from a bit of proverbial roughness round the edges: there is a certain truth, an honesty, there.

Your photo archive for today needs to include the impetuous moments but, more importantly, it needs to include simple, honest, straightforward portraits: of ourselves, our family, our home and our surroundings. As this is an archive for the future, the images need to be fully captioned: who they are of, where they are from, when they were taken, plus any other relevant details: 'on her seventieth birthday'; 'before the house was pulled down'; 'Millie's cousin'. If only our families had done just that in the past. How often do we hear, 'I've got all these photos but I don't know who they are of'?

Defining idea... **'A family's photograph album is generally about the extended family and, often, is all that remains of it.'**
SUSAN SONTAG (1933–2005) US author, critic

Think, too, about a three-, or even four-generation photograph. In fact, many of the best family photographs involve more than one person: the natural reaction between mother and child, grandma and grandpa, brother and sister is hard to cover up. Like so much in life, simplicity should be the overriding principle, so forget complicated backdrops and props. You are not wanting to be creative, so have a look in a few professional photographers' shop windows for ideas, or in the posh glossy magazines.

By collecting postcards of a specific place you can create a unique archive. Learn more from IDEA 48, *A rue with a view.*

Try another idea...

With the ease of taking photos has come the ability to seamlessly alter the content of a photograph and create a lie. Photo-manipulation programs allow you to do all sorts of wonderful things: remove blemishes, create graduation photos of those who never went to university, remove unwanted relatives from wedding groups and even add those who weren't there at all. Such an image is fake, it's a lie; it ceases to be a true record; it ceases to be any sort of record.

There is an argument that formal photographs tend to make us look at the subjects rather than into them, and that is a bad thing. Candid images need something to counterbalance them, without the overtones of emotion. Don't stop snapping away and capturing those irreplaceable moments. They have a very important place in our culture and our memories.

'You need to learn to see and compose. The more time you waste worrying about your equipment the less time you'll have to put into creating great images. Worry about your images, not your equipment.'
KEN ROCKWELL, photographer

Defining idea...

215

How did it go?

Q **Surely the 'formal' photograph can be as untypical as any other photograph. If I get my family to go out of their way to dress up and get their hair done specially, then this isn't really them either, is it?**

A *Quite right. The one major difference between what we need to do now and what our ancestors did is that we should remain as natural as possible. If you are usually seen in shirt and tie, then wear them; if jeans and T-shirt then those. The purpose is to capture an accurate likeness. The Victorian idea of not smiling was not so daft – we don't all go round with a supercilious grin on our faces all the time, do we?*

Q **I have tried taking a formal photo or two, but my family all look very self-conscious. I suppose it's because they are not used to it. Any suggestions?**

A *You could of course get a professional to do the work for you. Or you could follow the words of advice given as far back as 1849 by Henry Snelling: 'The conformation of the sitter should be minutely studied to enable you to place her or him in a position the most graceful and easy to obtain. The eyes should be fixed on some object a little above the camera, and to one side but never into, or on the instrument, as some direct; the latter generally gives a fixed, still, staring, scowling, or painful expression to the face.'*

50

Diversify – doing your own thing

There are plenty of opportunities to follow your own interests and keep your passion burning. Research what really fascinates you, not what the books tell you that you should be doing.

For many family historians, completing a family tree is only just the beginning. To just collect names and dates can be a very mundane and sterile activity (often likened to 'train spotting').

Your ultimate aim should be to gain information and understanding about your ancestors and the lives they led, firmly setting them into their own special place in history with the locations and time periods in which they lived. But, that doesn't mean you can't also search out anything that takes your fancy along the way.

It's important to allow yourself the freedom to study anything that captures your interest. Family historians are very much like any other detectives, piecing together

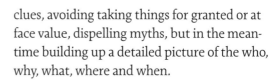

Here's an idea for you...

If you want to reach out to those interested in the same areas of research as yourself, try creating your own e-zine or blog (online diary). You could also circulate them to friends and family to keep them abreast of your latest findings.

clues, avoiding taking things for granted or at face value, dispelling myths, but in the meantime building up a detailed picture of the who, why, what, where and when.

This is a journey that can take you in any direction and as far as you desire – depending on exactly what your aims and objectives actually are and your appetite for the chase down the road of discovery. So what are your options and how can you realise them?

After a time, many of us become 'sidetracked' in our research, even if it's just a small diversion down a particular line of research to confirm a particular family story. You may want to discover if Bing Crosby was truly related to your father's family (as the story goes) or whether Great-Uncle Albert really did go to America and then on to Australia, and did he leave any descendants on the way, and how many wives did he have (at the same time).

You might have a major change of direction, caused by the fact that you cannot find your Great-Great-Great-Grandfather being born in the 1780s. Not to be defeated, you decide to collect information on everyone of that particular surname anywhere in the world – starting your very own one-name study. Or, of course, you may discover that as you move back in time the majority of your ancestors came from a specific place for which there doesn't seem to be very much documented information, so you may decide to do a one-place study. This may, of course, be the place that you now live in but with no actual relevance to your ancestry.

If your interests are growing in the role of your ancestors in the military, take a look at IDEA 25, *Daddy, what did you do in the war?* *Try another idea…*

Many of your ancestors may have been in the army or navy or been tinkers, tailors or spies, but what did they actually do; what did their daily work involve? Perhaps military or naval history has grasped your imagination. Or do you want to join the ranks of those organising specialist indexes of combmakers, lacemakers, gamekeepers, brickmakers or rat catchers and the like?

Perhaps you want to help other people with their research by becoming involved in a local or family history society. If there isn't one in your local area, see if anyone is interested in helping you organise a group. Or do you want to get involved in transcribing and indexing records – for example, parish registers or

'Imagination is a quality given a man to compensate him for what he is not, and a sense of humour was provided to console him for what he is.'
OSCAR WILDE (1854–1900)

Defining idea…

gravestones; newspapers with their obituaries, scandal, announcements, advertisements, sales particulars and so forth?

Or you could do a historical survey of your house, or an ancestor's house, or trace its history, researching the families that lived there and how they fitted into the history of the area or into your history. You might be interested in the development of education in an ancestor's village – perhaps you might like to help compile the history of your ancestor's school (if one's not been written already).

Researching your family history and honing your research skills can lead you to look beyond the family tree, exploring much further than discovering just who you think you are.

Q **Why is it so important to make sure that I fully document my research?**

How did it go?

A *Properly documenting and taking time to organise a research log, setting down when and where you found your information, will save time and effort later in your research. Without doing this, you are likely to look at those same sources again, only to find, or not find, what you already knew. One of the first things suggested to new researchers is to check 'what's been done before'. Documentation can help avoid duplication of research, especially when several people are researching the same lines. We make use of transcripts and indexes and thus depend on high-quality previous research to help us. Without documentation, we do not know what sources somebody has used and therefore what we are looking at. Remember: 'without proof, there is no truth'.*

Q **I'm interested in undertaking some research using some very old medieval records – which I'm not able to read. Where do I go from here?**

A *Seeking out the assistance of a professional genealogist can be prudent if you encounter a challenging research problem like this. They also know exactly where to locate specific records, and what they contain. A professional assessment of your 'case' can save a lot of wasted time, and often money. It's especially useful where the documents you require are not easy for you to access. There are several organisations (which operate under a code of practice) that can help you locate a professional researcher.*

51

Get Googling

The internet is a vast collection of information and it grows remorselessly by the day, by more than a million pages. To get the best from it, you need to learn to use it effectively.

One of the greatest misconceptions people have when beginning to undertake research online is the belief that it will all appear at a click or three of their mouse.

The internet is the largest repository of information in the world. And that is also its downside. Locating the valuable information that is out there to help us research our past can be a formidable task, particularly because as the amount of information grows, so the number of 'hits' increases when we undertake any search.

Searching the internet is like searching for the proverbial needle. However, remember that there are various ways to search the content of the internet and you can waste a lot less time chasing dead ends if you learn how to search more efficiently.

Search engines are the card indexes of the internet – searchable databases of websites collected by special programs called crawlers, spiders or robots. These scour the internet and index the text they contain into a very large database. There are many such search engines and each has different strengths when searching for different types of information. Among the more powerful search engines for research purposes are Google (www.google.com), Northern Light (www.northernlight.com), FASTSearch (www.alltheweb.com), Alta Vista (www.altavista.com), Ask (www.ask.com) and Vivisimo (http://vivisimo.com). Yahoo (www.yahoo.com) is slightly different, being a search directory rather than a search engine, but it is one of the largest guides to the web.

Undertaking a search using any of the search engines or directories appears to be very straightforward: you type in what you're looking for and click on the 'Search' or 'Go' button. The result: thousands of sites are returned. To work your way through this mass of information could take hours of valuable time. Possibly the first dozen or so entries may include what you want, and are the more likely to, but they may very well not. So, how can you make your searching more effective?

The judicious use of quotation marks is an essential part of successful internet searching. If you search for 'Brighton Palace Pier fire', using quotation marks, search engines will treat the words as an exact phrase and you will

Here's an idea for you...

Normally, when undertaking searches in online databases, less is more. In other words, you enter as little information as possible and only if there are too many results do you enter some additional data, and so forth, until the number of hits becomes manageable. It's the same with search engines, although here you will almost certainly have to start with a considered string of information. Try it. Just enter the name of an ancestor or place that interests you and note the number of hits, Then add some other relevant information: a town, an event, a subject such as 'history' or 'genealogy'. Try different combinations and some Boolean operators to see how the number of hits is affected and, hopefully, you'll become more centred around what you want.

get around 45 hits. If you don't use the quotation marks you will get over 38,000 hits.

You can also use what are called Boolean operators to undertake more complex and focused searches. The most important of these are AND, OR and NOT: instead of AND you can usually use '+', and for NOT use '-'. Therefore, using 'Palace Pier' + Brighton - fire will search for the exact phrase 'Palace Pier' with the word 'Brighton', but not the word 'fire', in the same article. Brackets can also be used together with the Boolean operators. '(Palace OR West) Pier' +Brighton, for example, will search for entries that include either 'Palace Pier' or 'West Pier' and the word 'Brighton'.

An asterisk '*' is used as a wild-card when making a search. It stands for one or more letters, or none. Some search engines require a minimum number of letters to the left of the asterisk, two or three. Therefore 'Robert*' will find 'Robert', 'Roberts', 'Robertson' and so forth. 'Wil*son' will find 'Wilson', 'Willson' and 'Wilkinson'.

Searching for information online is easy so long as you develop the mind and methods of a detective. You need to translate your problem into a language that can be used to search the internet: effectively, a series of key words and symbols. You could try something like 'Richard Spears' + (married OR marriage) + Sutton + Surrey. There are a number of useful keywords for genealogical searches apart from' genealogy' itself: ancestors, descendants, family history, birth/born, marriage/married, death/died.

You, too, can add to the mass of information available on the internet by having your own website. See IDEA 38, Publishing on the web.

Try another idea...

'The Internet is so big, so powerful and pointless that for some people it is a complete substitute for life.'
ANDREW BROWN

Defining idea...

'Basic research is what I am doing when I don't know what I am doing.'
WERNHER VON BRAUN
(1912–1977)

Defining idea...

Lastly, remember that there is sometimes a difference between UK English and US English, so watch your spelling: centre/center, labourer/laborer and the like.

How did it go?

Q Will my searches find information posted on newsgroups and e-mail groups?

A   *Mostly not. These need to be accessed directly once you know their URL, as do many online databases. These include such things as online telephone directories, image libraries, street directories and library catalogues. Google has a facility that allows you to search specific newsgroups, by subject or author.*

Q The family name I'm researching is Cook. You can guess what the problem is! What should I do?

A   *Yes! Make sure every search you make includes '- chef - food' (i.e. NOT chef, NOT food). If a celebrity shares the name you are searching for then make sure you remove them too – so, for example, 'Spears NOT Britney' is called for.*

How to avoid becoming an anorak

Being an avid history chaser doesn't mean you inevitably become the local bore who everybody avoids. Follow these simple rules and you can remain quite normal.

People with what seems to be an obsessive compulsion are often viewed with suspicion by others. So you need to retain the veneer of normality, no matter how exciting your research might be.

Many hobbies are group activities. For example, when going to football matches, you share the emotions, passions and experiences of watching a game with thousands of other people. And, of course, it's action packed – things are always changing and you have twenty-two players and their actions to discuss, plus, of course, the views and opinions of the commentators, and immediate feedback on the game via TV, radio, newspapers and specialist magazines. In contrast, the tere's an idea for you...

Find out where and when family or local history meeting or fairs are held near you. One thing you can be sure of is that all the people attending will be brimming with enthusiasm and keen to swap ideas. As a bonus, you might also find books and periodicals on sale that would never have otherwise come to your attention.

researching of your family history is generally a solitary occupation, with you as a single lone detective ploughing your way through a variety of records trying to fulfil your current goal or locate that elusive ancestor.

Researching the lives and times of your forebears, and the aspects of history that surrounded them, allows you to have a much deeper understanding of who you are, but there's the rub – it is who you are. As we are all unique individuals, each with our own ancestry, the minutest details of your family history are interesting and special to you, but only to you; you may be the only one who is fascinated and passionate about it. Very few of us are lucky enough to have all our ancestors leading action-packed lives that are interesting to the general populous. Sadly, most of my ancestors led fairly humdrum lives and most of their activities are certainly only of interest to me. This of course does not diminish the passion, importance and satisfaction that I feel about knowing about my family's past.

Researching your family tree is a great excuse for organising a family reunion, providing an ideal opportunity to renew or make family acquaintances. It's much better than waiting for a wedding or a funeral, which is often the only time that you might meet your cousins, and it offers you an environment where you can talk about your ancestors to people who will (probably) be interested in your quest. On top of that, you will also be able to catch up on the lives and times of your living relatives, putting the present family into perspective and capturing some oral history at the same time. Even here, though, you should apply a cardinal rule in avoiding anorak status – listen very carefully to people and gauge what interest they truly have in the subject.

Family trees and their notes can be difficult to interpret unless you thoroughly follow what you are looking at – which is not always easy to do. So, if you wish to update the different branches of your extended family regularly, then try and present the information in a con-cise and interesting format. If you have really whetted someone else's appetite, they can always ask you for more information or give you a helping hand with the research.

Get your artistic side into action and scrapbook your research. Using your imagination, you could compile an archive that would engage even the most prosaic family members. For sheer inspiration, see IDEA 40, *Creative scrapbooking*.

Try
another
idea...

Try to seek out like-minded people to communicate with in the extensive world of family and local history. People who have the same interests as you do will help you to extend your knowledge and expertise, plus you can share your experiences with them and enjoy celebrating each other's achievements. Making yourself knowl-edgeable in your field means that people will seek you out to ask for your help and advice. Get involved with your local society – even if you don't have any interests in the area – because you will be mixing with people who share your passion.

We are all different and enjoy different pastimes and activities. Some of us enjoy watching sport, reading books, climbing mountains or walking our dogs – and some of us enjoy researching our family and local history.

'You are never too old to set another goal or to dream a new dream.'
C. S. LEWIS (1898–1963) academic, writer and Christian apologist

Defining
idea...

How did it go?

Q   How can I try to get my husband and children interested in their family history?

A   *Try to do only very small bits of research while they are all with you so that they don't become too bored. For example, if you're out on a summer afternoon ramble, don't spend too long looking for family graves in the local graveyard. Doing some background work on your own before you go can help you quickly locate said graves – which is much more likely to impress and enthuse the rest of the family. However, you may just have to face the fact that although they may be interested in some of your discoveries, golf or computer games may have a higher priority in their lives.*

Q   How do I deal with relatives who have fixed ideas about their ancestry that do not seem to relate to the information I've gained through extensive research using primary resources?

A   *Usually when someone has very fixed ideas of 'the truth' about their family's ancestry, it is very difficult to persuade them to consider any other alternatives. I have a relative who is convinced that the family is descended from English royalty, even to the extent that they have changed their name to reflect their 'inherited status'. However, during my extensive research of that family, I have not been able to find any evidence to confirm this line of thought. So, until I do, I quietly treat it as an unconfirmed family story. I suggest you do the same.*

Brilliant resources

USEFUL CONTACTS AND WEBSITES

Access to Archives (catalogues of many national and local record offices and libraries)
www.a2a.org.uk
ARCHON (contact details for record repositories in the United Kingdom)
www.nationalarchives.gov.uk/archon
Association of Family History Societies of Wales
www.fhswales.info
British Association for Local History: PO Box 6549, Somersal Herbert, Ashbourne DE6 5WH
www.balh.co.uk
British History Online: (containing sources for the medieval and modern history of the British Isles)
www.british-history.ac.uk
British Library 96 Euston Road, London NW1 2DB
www.bl.uk
British Library Newspapers: Colindale Avenue, London NW9 5HE
www.bl.uk/catalogues/newspapers.html
College of Arms: Queen Victoria Street, London EC4V 4BT
www.college-of-arms.gov.uk
Commonwealth War Graves Commission: 2 Marlow Road, Maidenhead, Berkshire SL6 7DX
www.cwgc.org
Corporation of London Record Office: Joint Archives Service, 40 Northampton Road, London EC1R 0HB
www.cityoflondon.gov.uk/clro
County Histories (Victoria County History and links to county-based sources)
www.englandpast.net
Family Records (the official source for family records)
www.familyrecords.gov.uk
Family Records Centre: 1 Myddelton Street, London EC1R 1UW
www.familyrecords.gov.uk/frc
Federation of Family History Societies: PO Box 2425, Coventry CV5 6YX
www.ffhs.org.uk

Gazettes Online (*London, Edinburgh* and *Belfast Gazette*)
       www.gazettes-online.co.uk
General Register Office for England & Wales: Smedley Hydro, Trafalgar Road, Southport PR8 2HH
       www.gro.gov.uk/gro
   Public Search Room: Family Records Centre, 1 Myddelton Street, London EC1R 1UW
General Register Offices (Channel Islands)
   Jersey: Royal Court House, Royal Square, St Helier, Jersey JE2 4WA
       www.gov.je/judicialgreffe
   Guernsey: Alderney, Herm & Sark: H.M. Grefffier, The Royal Court House, St Peter Port, Guernsey
   GY1 2PB
General Register Office (Irish Republic) Government Offices, Convent Road, Roscommon
   Public Search Room: Joyce House, 8/11 Lombard Street East, Dublin, 2
       www.groireland.i.e.
General Register Office (Northern Ireland): Oxford House, 49–55 Chichester Street, Belfast BT1 4HL
   www.groni.gov.uk
General Register Office for Scotland: New Register House, 3 West Register Street, Edinburgh EH1 3YT
   www.gro-scotland.gov.uk
   (*see also* Scotland's People)
General Registry (Isle of Man): Isle of Man Courts of Justice, Deemsters Walk, Bucks Road, Douglas
   IM1 3AR
       www.gov.im/registries
Genuki (portal for British and Irish research)
       www.genuki.org.uk
Guildhall Library: Aldermanbury, London EC2P 2JE
       www.cityoflondon.gov.uk/guildhalllibrary
Guild of One-name Studies: Box G, 14 Charterhouse Buildings, Goswell Road, London EC1M 7BA
       www.one-name.org
Historical Directories (scanned images of selected trade directories)
       www.historicaldirectories.org
Historical Manuscripts Commission (*see* The National Archives)
House of Lords Record Office: Parliamentary Archives, London SW1A 0PW
       www.parliament.uk
Imperial War Museum: Lambeth Road, London SE1 6HZ
       www.iwm.org.uk
Moving Here (sources for migration to Britain)

www.movinghere.org.uk

The National Archives: Ruskin Avenue Kew, Richmond TW9 4DU
www.nationalarchives.gov.uk

National Archives of Ireland: Bishop Street, Dublin 8, Ireland
www.nationalarchives.i.e.

National Archives of Scotland: H M General Register House, Edinburgh EH1 3YY
www.nas.gov.uk
(*see also* Scotland's People)

National Army Museum: Royal Hospital Road, London SW3 3BU
www.national-army-museum.ac.uk

National Library of Wales: Aberystwyth, Ceredigion SY23 3BU
www.llgc.org.uk

National Maritime Museum: Greenwich, London SE10 9NF
www.nmm.ac.uk

National Monuments Record: Kemble Drive, Swindon SN2 2GZ
www.english-heritage.org.uk/nmr

National Monuments Record of Wales: Crown Building, Plas Crug, Aberystwyth SY23 1NJ
www.rcahmw.org.uk

National Monuments Records of Scotland: John Sinclair House, 16 Bernard Terrace, Edinburgh EH8 9NX
www.rcahms.gov.uk

Old Maps (downloadable old UK maps)
www.old-maps.co.uk

Parliamentary Archives (see House of Lords Record Office)

Principal Registry of the Family Division: First Avenue House, 42–49 High Holborn, London WC1V 6NP
www.hmcourts-service.gov.uk

Public Record Office of Northern Ireland: 66 Balmoral Avenue, Belfast BT9 6NY, Northern Ireland
www.proni.gov.uk

Scotland's People (the official government source for Scottish genealogical data)
www.scotlandspeople.gov.uk

Scottish Association of Family History Societies
www.safhs.org.uk

Society of Genealogists: 14 Charterhouse Buildings, London EC1M 7BA
www.sog.org.uk

The end...

Or is it a new beginning?

We hope the ideas in this book will have inspired you to try some new things to unearth your heritage. Perhaps you've already organised a family reunion to dig up some secrets, joined your local history society or gone on a sleuthing expedition round your town. The insights in this book should have helped you organise your information, learn to plan and hone your investigational skills.

So why not let *us* know all about it? Tell us how you got on. What did it for you – what really helped you shine a light on the past? Maybe you've got some tips of your own you want to share (see next page if so). And if you liked this book you may find we have even more brilliant ideas that could change other areas of your life for the better.

You'll find the Infinite Ideas crew waiting for you online at www.infideas.com.

Or if you prefer to write, then send your letters to:
Discover your roots
The Infinite Ideas Company Ltd
36 St Giles, Oxford, OX1 3LD, United Kingdom

We want to know what you think, because we're all working on making our lives better too. Give us your feedback and you could win a copy of another *52 Brilliant Ideas* book of your choice. Or maybe get a crack at writing your own.

Good luck. Be brilliant.

Offer one

CASH IN YOUR IDEAS

We hope you enjoy this book. We hope it inspires, amuses, educates and entertains you. But we don't assume that you're a novice, or that this is the first book that you've bought on the subject. You've got ideas of your own. Maybe our author has missed an idea that you use successfully. If so, why not put it in an email and send it to: yourauthormissedatrick@infideas.com, and if we like it we'll post it on our bulletin board. Better still, if your idea makes it into print we'll send you four books of your choice. or the cash equivalent. You'll be fully credited so that everyone knows you've had another Brilliant Idea.

Offer two

HOW COULD YOU REFUSE?

Amazing discounts on bulk quantities of Infinite Ideas books are available to corporations, professional associations and other organisations.

For details call us on:
+44 (0)1865 514888
fax: +44 (0)1865 514777
or e-mail: info@infideas.com

Where it's at ...

adultery, 32, 33
apprenticeships and
    apprentices, 123–126, 128:
    migration, 95; parish chests,
    138–139
architectural research, 193–196
archives, 77–81: creating your
    own, 8, 48, 177–180, 213–216;
    directories, 61, 62
armed forces, 114–122
auction houses, online, 15

banns registers, 94, 99
baptismal registers, 99–100, 128
beating-of-the-bounds, 208
bigamy, 32, 33, 34
biographies, 133–134
birth certificates and records,
    10, 27–30, 70–71: addresses,
    and electoral registers,
    66; censuses, 57, 58;
    nonconformists, 110–111;
    professionals' children,
    134
Bishop's Transcripts, 98, 101
Books of Remembrance, 49
British Army, 115, 119, 120:
    schools, 52
British Library: charters, 78;
    directories, 62; newspapers,
    39, 54; occupations, 130; Poll
    Books, 68; professions and
    professionals, 134; school
    records, 54

burial grounds, 173–176:
    memorials, 47–50, 175
burial registers and records,
    71, 94, 176: cause of death,
    42, 45; and gravestones,
    cross-checking between, 49;
    nonconformists, 48, 111, 112;
    parish registers, 100

capital crimes, 149–150
cemeteries, 173–176:
    memorials, 49, 175
census records, 55–58; death
    indexes, 29; occupations,
    129, 130; professionals,
    134; school records, 54;
    separation, evidence of, 32
churches and churchyards:
    burials, 47–48, 49, 173–174;
    memorials, 47–48, 49; parish
    chests, 137–140; parish
    registers, 97–101; plans, 50;
    taxes, 70; voluntary schools,
    52; wills, 103, 106
churchwardens, 138, 140
civic heraldry, 143
civil registration, 27–30
coats-of-arms, 48, 141–144
College of Arms, 48, 142
Commonwealth War Graves
    Commission, 117
computers: scanning
    techniques, 76, 165–168;
    virtual scrapbooks, 180

coroners' inquests and records,
    42, 43–44, 45
Court Baron, 147
Court Leet, 146–147
crematoria and cremation,
    49, 174
criminal records, 149–152

Dame schools, 52, 54
dating practices, 89–92
death certificates and records,
    10, 27–30: addresses,
    and electoral registers,
    66; cause of death,
    41–42, 45; censuses, 29, 57;
    nonconformists, 110–111;
    occupations, 128
deaths: newspaper reports, 37,
    154; unusual, 41–45
desertion, 32, 33
directories: genealogical, 14;
    local, see local directories
divorce, 31–34
DNA testing, 161–164
Domesday Book, 70: Lloyd
    George Domesday survey,
    185–188, 198

education records, 51–54, 133
electoral registers, 65–68
emigration, 153–156: newspaper
    reports, 38; transportation,
    152
e-zines, 170–171, 218

family societies, 21–25, 229:
monumental inscriptions,
49–50; palaeography, 87;
strays indexes, 96; taxation
records, 72
Field Books, 187, 188
First World War, 113–117, 156
Freeholders Registers, 66, 68

genetic research, 161–164
gravestones and grave-boards,
47–48: and burial registers,
cross-checking between, 49;
missing, 50; suspicious, 50
graveyards, 173–176: memorials,
47–50, 175
Gregorian calendar, 89–91
Guildhall Library:
apprenticeships,
124; directories, 62;
nonconformists, 112; Poll
Books, 68

handwriting, deciphering old,
87, 146
Hearth Money, 70, 199
heraldry, 48, 141–144
heritage albums, 177–180, 229
house history: architectural
research, 193–196; Lloyd
George Domesday survey,
185–188; National Farm
Survey, 189–192; plots and
plans, 197–200

illegitimate children, 33, 100
immigration, 48, 157–160

Imperial War Museum, 114, 120
International Genealogical
Index (IGI), 94, 110, 152
internet and World Wide Web,
223–226: publishing on the,
169–172; scanned images,
167

Julian calendar, 89, 90–91

Kelly's directories, 60, 61

landscape history, 205–208:
postcards, 209–212
libraries, 79–81
Lloyd George Domesday survey,
185–188, 198
local directories, 59–63:
migration, 95; occupations,
129; professionals, 134
local history societies, 21–25,
229: house history, 200;
palaeography, 87; parish
studies, 138; taxation
records, 72
'lost' relatives: approaching,
18–19, 20; locating, 13

mailing lists, 16, 170
manorial documents, 145–148,
182
Manorial Documents Register,
147–148, 182
maps, 73–76
marriage certificates and
records, 10, 27–30, 71
medals, 10, 116, 117, 122

memorabilia, family, 9–12;
photographs, 201–204
memorials, 47–50
memories: family papers and
memorabilia, 9; oral history,
5–8
migration, 93–96, 140 see also
emigration; immigration
monumental inscriptions,
47–50, 174

names, see surnames
National Archives, The (TNA),
77–79, 81: apprenticeships,
124, 125, 128; armed forces,
120, 121, 122; criminal
records, 151; emigrants, 154,
156; First World War, 115,
116, 117; immigrants, 159;
Lloyd George Domesday
survey, 186, 187; manorial
documents, 148, 182;
National Farm Survey, 190,
192; nonconformists, 111;
palaeography, 87, 148; police
officer records, 152; wills, 104
National Farm Survey, 189–192,
198: maps, 75, 190, 191
newspapers, 35–39: births,
marriages and deaths, 28;
crimes, 150; emigrants, 154,
155; First World War, 115;
obituaries, 154; occupations,
129; school records, 54;
unusual deaths, 43, 45
nonconformists, 109–112:
baptismal registers, 100;

education, 52; monumental inscriptions, 48

occupations, 127–130: *see also* professions and professionals; tradespeople
one-name studies, 14, 25, 96, 181–183, 184: DNA testing, 163
one-place studies, 183, 184
oral history, 5–8, 17–20, 228–229
Ordnance Survey maps, 74–75, 76: house history, 198

palaeography (reading old handwriting), 87, 146
papers, family, 9–12
parish chests, 125, 137–140
parish registers, 99–101, 137, 140: emigrants, 155
passport records, 156
perpetual calendars, 90
photographs: aerial, 206–207; creating your own archive, 8, 48, 213–216; family, 201–204; of gravestones, 48; immigrants, 159; of properties, 194, 196
Poll Books, 65–68
postcards, 209–212
Prerogative Court of Canterbury (PCC), 104
prisons, 150
probate records, 103–107, 195: occupations, 129

professions and professionals, 131–135: *see also* occupations
property surveys: Lloyd George Domesday survey, 185–188; National Farm Survey, 189–192
Public Schools, 51, 54

Quakers, 111
Quarter days, 92
Quarter Sessions records: crimes, 150–151; occupations, 129; taxation, 72

ragged schools, 52, 54
record offices, 77–81: apprenticeships, 125; cemetery records, 176; directories, 61–62; electoral registers, 68; farm records, 192; house history, 198; Lloyd George Domesday survey, 186, 17; manorial documents, 148; maps and plans, 74, 76; migration, 95; nonconformists, 112; parish chests, 139; Quarter Sessions and Petty Sessions records, 150–151; wills, 105, 106; *see also* archives
removal orders, 95, 140
reunions, family, 7, 8, 228

school records, 51–54
scrapbooks, 177–180: scanned images, 167
search engines and search directories, 223–226
Second World War, 189–192
settlement certificates, 95, 140
Sheriff's Lists, 66, 68
spelling variations and errors, 3, 4, 58
stories, family, 5–8, 17–20
surnames, 1–4: networking, 15, 16; one-namers, 14, 25, 96, 163, 181–183, 184; spelling variations and errors, 3, 4, 58

tax records, 69–72: house history, 199; Lloyd George Domesday survey, 185, 186–187
telephone directories, 62
tradespeople, 127–130: apprenticeships, 123–126; directories of, 59–62
transportation, 152

Voters Lists, 66, 67, 68

wife-selling, 33
wills, 103–107
Window Tax, 70, 199
workhouse schools, 52, 54

Practical Family History or *Family Tree Magazine*

for all *Discover your roots* readers

We've teamed up with ABM Publishing Ltd, the UK's premier publisher of family history magazines to bring you the best possible advice on tracing your family history. *Discover your roots* contains all the tips and techniques to make the process of tracing your ancestry easy and fun. To get even more helpful advice why not choose your FREE copy from the two magazines detailed below to help you on the wonderful journey of exploring your heritage.

Family Tree Magazine was first published in 1984 and is the best selling British family history magazine. It's jam-packed with features written by leading personalities in the world of family history. Each issue includes articles on indexes, libraries and other resources, military history, social history and a question and answer section. Read reviews of the latest books, software CDs and websites and learn how to get the most out of your computer for family history research. Check out the website at: *www.family-tree.co.uk*

Practical Family History is ideal for those of you who are new to family history. Sources are simply and fully explained by leading writers on family history. Each issue explains how to use resources, including the internet, expert photo dating and interpretation, social history features and advice on using your computer for family history research. Write to PFH Answers and get your family history questions answered by their team of experts. There are plenty of special offers and regular giveaways up for grabs! Check out the website at: *www.practicalfamilyhistory.co.uk*

To find out more about these magazines or to purchase books, charts, binders, CD wallets and over 1,000 genealogical items you can go to the website at *www.familyhistorybookshop.co.uk*

To claim your FREE *Family Tree Magazine* or *Practical Family History* cut out or copy the coupon on this page, ticking the box to indicate which magazine you would prefer to receive and send to the address below. The latest available issue of the magazine will be sent to you.*

✂ ....

Please send me a FREE copy of my chosen magazine selected below

Practical Family History   ▢

Family Tree Magazine   ▢

Name: ....

Address: ....

....

....

....

Email: ....

Daytime Tel: ....

Please send to: ABM Magazine Offer, ABM Publishing Ltd, 61 Great Whyte, Ramsey, Cambridgeshire, PE26 1HJ

You may be contacted by Infinite Ideas or ABM publishing with news or other offers which may interest you. If you prefer not to be contacted please tick here[†] ▢

*On receipt of this order, your chosen magazine should be dispatched to you within 10 working days
[†]We never give details to third parties nor will we bombard you with lots of junk mail!